Black Champion

Black Champion

The Life and Times of Jack Johnson

Finis Farr

CHARLES SCRIBNER'S SONS

New York

Acknowledgments

I owe a debt of gratitude to John Durant, author of *The Heavyweight Champions* and student of Jack Johnson's career, for material from his files and for his kind interest in the writing of this book. Thanks also are due the editors of *Sports Illustrated* for permission to use passages that first appeared in their magazine in different form; and to their researchers in Galveston, Washington, and Chicago. In some measure the story of Johnson is also an account of the last-named city, and I am under a compounding debt to Wayne Andrews for *Battle for Chicago,* and Herbert Asbury for *Gem of the Prairie.* Johnson's memoirs are *Mes Combats,* published in Paris, and *Jack Johnson In the Ring and Out.* As in the case of any public figure, his version of events must be compared with contemporary accounts and supplemented by material from documentary collections. For indispensable aid of this kind, I am grateful to the director and staff of the Newberry Library in Chicago, the publisher and reference staff at the *Chicago Tribune,* the librarians at Time Incorporated, Mr. Robert H. Land at the Library of Congress, Miss Barbara D. Simison at the Yale University Library, and Mr. Robert W. Henderson, librarian at the Racquet and Tennis Club in New York.

—F.F.

Contents

Black Champion

I

Lonesome Blues

Jack Johnson was the first Negro to win the heavyweight professional boxing championship of the world. This feat made Johnson the most famous of all Negro boxers, although he was not the first member of his race to achieve eminence in the prize ring, nor the first to go abroad in search of competition. The original black professionals in North America were slaves whose owners backed them with bets; and among plantation champions the most successful was Tom Molineaux of Virginia, whose father had been a boxing slave before him. Weighing more than two hundred pounds and built low and wide, this formidable man won his freedom in the ring, went to New York and then to England, and challenged the British champion Tom Cribb in 1809. Molineaux lost to Cribb, though some historians say it was by a fraudulent decision. But whether or not he was cheated in that match, Molineaux showed how prize fighting could be the means by which a man of his color might gain prominence and a certain undeniable importance akin to that of a theatrical star. Through the years that followed, many Negroes tried it and some earned money and fame; but none approached the success that Johnson enjoyed in the days when he stood at the height of his career and the top of his profession. And by the same token, none of them had to suffer so hard an ultimate fall.

He was born in Galveston, Texas, on March 31, 1878. We can therefore easily calculate that fifteen years separated John Arthur Johnson at his birth from the days of slavery, if we count its end with Mr. Lincoln's Proclamation; or reckoning from the passage of the Thirteenth Amendment, it was thirteen years. Only two years had passed since the end of the Reconstruction period, during which Southern Negroes had wielded heavy political influence under the protection of Federal troops dispatched from Washington. Now that was over for a while; over forever, most people thought, with Rutherford B. Hayes in the White House reforming the civil service and working for the solidification of American currency into gold. Brought to office after an election so close that it had to be settled in Congress, Hayes was conciliatory toward the South; and not only there, but everywhere in the country, the Negro was ushered to a back seat. Few white people questioned this ordering of affairs; and only the most able and gifted Negroes rose above it. At the time of Johnson's birth, the best-known Negro in the country was Frederick Douglass, who had escaped from slavery to become an abolitionist editor and speaker. With the great cause won, Douglass settled to the writing of his autobiography; as an international celebrity, he seemed almost like a foreigner to the humble Negroes on the Galveston waterfront.

Jack Johnson's father was a pious man who earned the family living as janitor of a school. The older Johnson had so sturdy a religious conviction that he often appeared at camp meetings to help the professional clergy in marathons of preaching to communicants whose concentration on the gospel was so intense that they gave spoken approval to each point. Later in life Johnson was to show considerable verbal agility, an adroitness acquired from listening to this sort of preaching.

Some of Johnson's Galveston childhood is on record, and part of it can be reconstructed from the memories of surviving citizens. But we would do well to bear in mind a remark made in 1955 by Roi Ottley, biographer of Robert S. Abbot, founder of the *Chicago Defender* and one of the first American Negroes to become a millionaire. Organizing the ascertainable facts of his subject's early life, Ottley wrote, "Until now, most Negroes who have achieved anything noteworthy seemingly have no traceable background." Johnson had respectable and known parentage, but many questions cannot be answered. For example, had Johnson's father been a slave? Nobody knows. He may have been one of the 488,070 free Negroes in the South before the Civil War.* It would seem that he was not one of the four thousand or more Negroes who themselves owned slaves,** nor was he, apparently, one of the thrifty and fortunate Negroes who owned land. No evidence can be found that Johnson's father ever had a trade, which is perhaps the strongest argument for the theory that he had been a slave before the war. But

* This figure is from Dr. Carter G. Woodson, *The Negro in Our History*.
** According to Dr. John Hope Franklin, whose researches show at least this number of Negroes owning slaves in 1869.

whatever the facts of Johnson's family economic history there is one question on which we can be certain: his biological heritage was pure African, of the strong and healthy Coromantee stock.

Johnson's mother was an intelligent woman, well thought of in the North Side neighborhood where he was born. Her given name of Tina was corrupted into "Tiny," starting the legend that she was unusually small. This was not true—Tina Johnson was of average size. Another myth perpetuated in the newspapers had it that Jack gained his neighborhood nickname of "Little Arthur" because he had been an abnormally small child. On the contrary, he had been a big baby, growing at the usual rate into a big boy and a big man, standing six feet two inches and weighing a little over two hundred pounds at the height of his professional career.

That career was founded on an inborn genius for fast movement, a gift that Johnson did not recognize until about his thirteenth year. Up to that time he left fighting to his brother Henry, or to his three sisters, whose names were Lucy, Fannie, and Jane. When Johnson discovered his speed he found that along with it he had been endowed with an easy natural boxing style. One gift complemented the other, so that sixty years later a friend remembered, "Jack was so fast he could block a punch and hit you with the same hand."

A couple of years after he became aware of his boxing talent, Jack left school to find work. He had finished the fifth grade, which was little enough formal instruction; at that, his handwriting was legible and he could read with ease.

Jack's first job was on a milk wagon, at a salary of $1.25 per week; he soon bettered himself by joining the staff of Gregory's Livery Stables. His duties were to exercise the horses, and to take them around to the customers. A boyish love of action sometimes led him into overexercising the animals and passing them on to clients as exhausted as though they had just been used to bring the good news from Ghent to Aix. On discovery of this, the boss cursed Johnson, and told him to stay away on pain of complaint to the police. Nor was it taken as a valid excuse when Johnson said he had only been imitating Isaac Murphy, the Negro jockey who was the greatest rider on the American track.

After this episode, Johnson's parents were relieved when the boy found a quiet job as apprentice in a bakery. He showed intelligence by learning the rudiments of the trade in a short time. All his life, he could make bread and plain cake, and this ability was to come in handy at another period, as we shall see. Tiring of the baker's shop, he left it for a job that demanded more from his muscles while putting more in his pocket, as a longshoreman on the Galveston docks.

The first day on the docks, Johnson's mates warned him of a bully who thrashed all who failed to pay tribute. Too proud to admit he was broke, Johnson said a fight would be agreeable to him. The bully made one charge—and was carried home with a steel hook in his right deltoid muscle. Some who saw the fight remained to marvel at the swiftness of Johnson's counterattack; others ran to tell Tiny, where she sat on the porch shelling peas while two scrawny chickens pecked the dirt. When Jack got home, his parents reproached him, for they knew this kind of fighting could be deadly. All the boy would say was, "Tough times make tough people."

At intervals Jack would work at Professor Herman Bernau's Sporting Gymnasium. He was not an instructor; his duty was to keep the place clean. Professor Bernau allowed Johnson to punch the bag after hours, and exercise with the weights and pulleys. Jack also had the privilege of buying two pairs of boxing gloves at the wholesale price. He carried these gloves around the Negro section of Galveston, always taking them along when he strolled to the corner of Eleventh Street and Avenue K, three blocks from his house, where the colored sporting men, boozers, and petty thieves liked to congregate.

At this gathering place Johnson would walk up to a man, throw him one pair of the gloves, and start pulling on the other. This was the signal for an informal boxing bout in which Jack always delighted the spectators, while rapidly taking the heart out of his opponent. A friend recalled, "He could predict every blow. He'd tell you he was going to hit you in the eye, and he would. He'd say he was going to hit you in the mouth, and he would. He was the most scientific fighter the world ever produced."

Confronted by this type of science, which might be more accurately defined as superlative instinctive skill, the loungers of Avenue K decided to accept no more of Johnson's challenges.

"Take those things away, Little Arthur," a man would say, recoiling from the proffered gloves as though they were made of red-hot metal. "I ain't no punching bag."

Partly because of the scarcity of worthy opposition in

boxing, and also because of the unrest of youth, Johnson began to range the country, from coast to coast. He did this by way of the freight trains that were available to anyone reckless enough to board them, and nimble enough to avoid the brakemen, who were known as "shacks," and the railroad police. In this manner Johnson cheated the railroads of the fare for thousands of miles, and was lucky enough not to leave an arm or leg behind him, as many a young fellow did when he slipped beneath a train, or when shacks or hostile hoboes threw him there. He was not so lucky begging handouts in the railroad towns, where he frequently encountered sheriffs who arrested him for vagrancy and locked him in jail.

Sometimes there was music in prison. The white vagrants soothed Johnson's ears with their ballads of loss and shame, but he liked best to hear a voice that seemed distinctively that of his own people in the lonesome blues. Stretched on the cot and looking at the ceiling ho would listen:

> Good mornin', blues,
> Blues, how do you do?
> Yes, blues, how do you do?
> Blues say, I'm all right,
> Good mornin', how are you?
> Woke up this mornin'
> Blues all around my head—
> Walked in to eat my breakfast,
> I had the blues all in my bread.
>
> For how long? How long?
> I say, how long?

Though the days in prison seemed to have no end, the total confinement in each case was seldom more than a week, for the jailings were merely to discourage the return of undesirable persons, as the officers made clear when releasing the vagrants, adding emphasis to their warnings with a few blows and kicks. But no lawman ever impressed Johnson so much as a town marshal in Idaho, who said, as he unlocked the jailhouse door, "Boy, if I ever see you again, I'm going to shoot you in the head, and then put a pistol in your hand."

Johnson headed East and eight nights later walked the streets of New York City for the first time. Here he gratified a wish to see Steve Brodie, the hero of an alleged jump into the East River from the Brooklyn Bridge. After looking at Brodie, who was now running a saloon, Johnson beat his way to Boston, where he found work as an exercise boy at the stables near the racetrack. His salary was five dollars a week, plus bed and board. He augmented this wage by steady winning at the dice game in the grooms' quarters. Johnson was a shrewd gambler, who early in life grasped the principle that in craps, the odds are against the shooter. By covering the bets of those who thought otherwise, Johnson built up a fat little bank roll, which he protected from theft by letting his colleagues know that he carried a knife. Johnson did well against all human opposition during this period; defeat overtook him because of a vicious horse.

This animal chose Jack as an enemy, and would stamp and kick at the sound of his voice. Johnson believed he could move faster than any horse, and one cold morning allowed himself to be caught off guard. The cunning brute feigned good temper as Johnson entered the stall, and then kicked him into the gangway, where he lay unconscious; when the other stablehands picked Johnson up, it was found that he had a broken leg. So ended Johnson's career as a horseman; the dice bank roll barely sufficed to buy a ticket back to Galveston, and he got home convinced that in the North not only the sheriffs but even the animals were against him.

The break in Johnson's femur was clean, and healed so well that he was able to astonish the loungers on Avenue K by jumping ten feet backward from a standing start. Again the inscrutable processes of Johnson's luck may be noted: if the iron on the horse's hoof had struck a knee instead of the thighbone, he might have ended his days on the docks.

Untroubled by any notion that his case might be cited in developing a theory of fortuitous history, Johnson began to think about making money from his quickness of foot and his ability to strike a paralyzing blow with either hand. At this time, the Bob Tomlinson affair took place, and it is worth noting. Tomlinson was a professional boxer turned circus roustabout, traveling through Texas in that spring of 1897 with a carnival troupe, and picking up easy money by fighting all comers in a tented ring. With spectators at fifty cents a head, Tomlinson offered five dollars to anyone who could stay four rounds with him. Few of the farm boys, ranch hands, and saloon fighters who tried for this prize survived even one round, and none had ever been upright at the end of four, but Tomlinson's victories were not invariably due to professional skill. When faced by an able competitor, he would shoulder his man against a canvas curtain, behind which lurked a colleague who knocked the challenger unconscious by slapping a blackjack across the curve of his skull. As the victim's knees buckled, Tomlinson would add a couple of punches to make the thing look right. By such methods, this hardened rogue had poleaxed some of the stoutest amateur bruisers in Texas; but retribution caught him on a vacant lot in the outskirts of Galveston, when Jack Johnson accepted his invitation to enter the ring.

As Johnson climbed through the ropes, Tomlinson sized him up as stupid but strong. Accordingly he flashed a signal known as "the office" for his confederate to take position behind the screen. A gong sounded. Johnson came from his corner in a loose-jointed, shuffling way that caught the attention of the audience and roused professional interest in Bob Tomlinson. He decided to keep Johnson going for three rounds to please the crowd.

It was not by sufferance that Johnson survived the three rounds: if anyone was carried along, it was Tomlinson. Jack avoided his rushes with ease, or tied him up at close quarters, smiling all the while with the kindly air of a dining-car attendant or a Pullman porter. At the start of the fourth round, Tomlinson tried to bull Johnson into the curtain and finish him off. But Jack refused to be crowded, tossed Tomlinson halfway across the ring, bounded after him, and whipped over a belly punch that made his eyes bug out. Bent and gasping, the caved-in Tomlinson was barely able to give the office for the timekeeper to tap the gong. And the five dollars Jack thereupon collected were the first that he earned with his fighting skill.

This early triumph of Jack Johnson had the authentic stamp of his swift reactions. A stimulus arriving in Johnson's cortex did not linger, but was instantly off to the required part of his body. The high tuning of his nervous system owed something to brawls on the Galveston waterfront against enemies armed with knives and bailing hooks, and something to reflexes acquired in jumping off boxcars and escaping through freight yards when pursued by railroad cops carrying metal-weighted clubs. It should also go on record that the bout in which he flattened the showman demonstrated a feature of Johnson's showmanship: while working he always liked to chat with the crowd, radiating benevolence and an air of negligent mastery that implied his only purpose was to show that no one could hurt him in the ring. Virtuosity was there for anyone in the small audience under the tent to see; and shortly after this appearance, Johnson got a match at the Galveston Athletic Club.

The members of the club called the bouts "exhibition contests" because it was illegal to stage a prize fight as such. Here Johnson met and defeated a fighter known as "the Galveston Giant," receiving a few dollars for the win. During the following year he took part on three occasions in a battle royal. This form of contest had six men enter the ring and swing away until only one was on his feet. Though open to criticism on grounds of humanity, such bouts could hardly be improved on as a toughening process.

Jack Johnson had a fidgety foot, and after a few more semi-professional fights in Galveston he was off again, riding the brake rods to St. Louis under the fast freight, as pieces of gravel shot from the roadbed and tore holes in his coat. Next he beat his way to Florida, where he shipped aboard a coral fisherman's boat. One day on the first cruise, while the boat was rolling through blue water, Johnson saw a monstrous shark swim alongside. He vowed the creature was nineteen feet long, and that it was looking at him with a hungry expression in its eyes. When he went aft, the shark followed, lifting its jaws and snapping at him. The coral captain gave the shark a blast with a shotgun, and when they hauled it aboard, the tail lashed at Johnson in the death throes. He made his backward leap as he was used to doing it in Galveston, but there was blood on the deck; he slipped and cracked a rib.

The horse in Boston, now this thing from Florida water —Johnson wanted to know, looking at the dull-gray hide of the dead shark, if the entire natural order was arrayed against him. The captain did not think so, and pointed out that the shark was only six feet long, but throughout his life, Johnson gave it extra measure. In this, as in all other matters, accuracy was the least of his worries.

When Johnson got on shore, he took off by freight train for Chicago. There he visited the camp of the West Indian Negro welterweight Joe Walcott, a skilled, graceful fighter known as "the Barbados Demon." Walcott gave Johnson his first employment as a professional boxer in a recognized troupe by adding him to the corps of sparring partners. Payment was in lodging and board, the latter a considerable item, for Johnson had by this time developed a trait which would be with him all his life—a capacity for food in large quantities. Breakfasting at Walcott's training table, Johnson would call for "a setting of eggs and a skillet of pork chops." The cook never quite filled this order, but if he had, Johnson would have put it away. He was a big enough eater to cause talk of matching him against one of the professional gluttons who performed at the time in saloons and chop-houses. Some of the sparring partners went so far as to start negotiations to put Johnson against an eater who billed himself as "the Great Consumo," for a purse of fifty dollars, plus side bets, but the match fell through when Consumo died of a surfeit. Thereafter, Johnson's common sense kept him from such stomach-bursting recklessness. All the same, Walcott's food did him a world of good.

He also picked up from "the Barbados Demon" a West Indian accent that he could adapt at will, and would occasionally use at later periods to astonish his auditors when on the lecture platform or speaking from the pulpit. But the best thing Walcott did for Johnson was to polish his fighting style. With his own natural rhythm, the Demon was a fine instructor for Johnson, teaching him graceful movement that was a kind of art. It is true that the clumsiest fighter can rise to the top of his trade, so long as he knocks other men down. Johnson knew this, but throughout his long professional life—he was still giving exhibitions at the age of sixty-eight—he was proud that, in addition to power, he had style.

Shortly after joining the troupe, Jack appeared before the Chicago public in opposition to the experienced Negro heavyweight known as Klondike, who knocked Johnson cold in the fifth round—one of the three defeats by knockout that seem ascertainable in Johnson's record.* This

---

* In his later career, Johnson knocked out Klondike three times. The other knockouts that Johnson received came from Joe Choyniski and Jess Willard.

rough treatment gave Johnson the idea that he would do well to return to Galveston and rest for a while, then rise and fight again. He assured Walcott he was not giving up the ring; and the Demon replied, "Mawn, you'd be a fool if you did—you with money in either hawnd."

Back in Galveston, Johnson decided it was time he took a wife, and united himself with a Negro girl named Mary Austin. Willing to see the world beyond Galveston, Mary went with him on his travels, making her first trip when he started on a tour of the country in 1899. Johnson joined a company of boxers who faced each other over and over in matches on which it was agreed that there should be no decision, and this is one reason why his fighting record is as difficult to put down with certainty as are some of the episodes in his life outside the ring.

Klondike was a member of the troupe, along with boxers who carried such ring names as Black Bill and Mexican Pete. Sometimes the athletes lived under canvas, and while they were camping it was not Mary, but Johnson himself who acted as cook. After all, he had been a baker, and in time to come his colleagues would recall his light hand with the flapjack dough. Johnson relished this duty, reasoning that if the cook went hungry it would be his own fault. Although conditions on this trip were mostly agreeable, the traveling fighters were not always able to accommodate one another in the ring. An example was the night in Cripple Creek when Johnson was matched with Mexican Pete before a crowd of drunken miners.

"Fight, Jack," Pete said as they clinched in the first round. "Those miners have pistols." In the twentieth round, Pete fell victim to an authentic knockout. Jack did well and saved money on this tour, but Mary went back to Galveston ahead of him, and they never lived together again.

On the twentieth of October, 1900, Johnson was riding a bicycle along the Galveston waterfront about five o'clock in the hot and sultry afternoon. Galveston is on an island, and, as Johnson looked across at the mainland, he saw that a curtain of dust had given a yellowish tone to the air. He later recalled that "everything felt heavy and dead." Then he heard people running, and saw a crowd of them rushing toward him through the murk, shouting as they ran.

"The Market Street Bridge is out!" yelled the fugitives. Then Johnson heard the hideous rending sound of the bridge collapsing—and next came a wind that blew him off his bicycle. A friend named Jack Marling pulled him to his feet, and screamed in his ear through the wind, "Your house is under water!"

Johnson turned and saw the ocean poised over the causeway that connected Galveston to the mainland. A number of sheet-iron roofs went sailing over Jack's head, while at his feet thousands of rats poured through the gutters. Johnson ran toward his house, falling a second time as a cloudburst hit him with a torrent of rain that turned to hail. He found his father lying in the street. The crowd was trampling the old man, and nearly killed him before Johnson managed to get him on his back and struggle to high ground. Later Johnson found the other members of his family—they had all escaped. But more than five thousand were not so lucky, and death took them either by trampling, drowning, or fire. Throughout the following week, Johnson saw the smokes of vast funeral pyres, and helped load the ships that put out for mass burials at sea.

Such was that great catastrophe, the Galveston tidal wave and flood. Thinking it over, Johnson concluded that Texas was not a good place to be just then. This was not because of superstition; the stereotype of the comic Negro caressing his rabbit's foot did not fit Jack Johnson. But he could play a hunch as well as the next man. Accordingly, he returned to Chicago, and here he met with hard times. A bitter cold winter came on; Johnson solved the problem of shelter by billeting himself as a non-paying guest in the meager South Side lodging of a Negro boxer named Frank Childs. There was a roof over their heads, but the more Johnson and Childs hunted work at their trade, the colder grew the managers and promoters, and the icier the waters of Lake Michigan. They walked so many miles looking for employment that Johnson said to Childs, "The soles of my shoes are worn so thin, I could step on a dime and tell you whether it was heads or tails." Johnson was able to eat because of credit extended by Walt Brothers, proprietor of a boarding house that was unusual in that it served only one meal a day. But Johnson ate well at this one meal: the first item would be a dozen hot biscuits drenched in butter; then came five glasses of milk, a steak, and for dessert a platter of lamb chops. Sad to say, Johnson never paid his debts to the man who set this bountiful table.

Yet just as Johnson bilked Walt Brothers, so his supposed friend Childs made trouble for Johnson. It happened that Childs was married, though separated from his wife, and had not told Johnson about it. Because of this, an unhappy event occurred on a night in the depth of winter. Years later, when Johnson wrote his memoirs in Paris under the title *Mes Combats,* he was still indignant about it. What happened was that Mrs. Childs returned to her husband's one-room residence late one miserably cold night, and Childs made Johnson leave. He spent the rest of the night near the lakefront huddled against the base of the statue that memorializes Senator Stephen A. Douglas. For hours he trembled with the cold, and suffered mental agonies through fear of catching pneumonia, which was often fatal in those days. The following year, Jack humiliated Childs in the ring, calling out blows before delivering them, knocking the arm aside whenever Frank tried to land a punch and hitting him with the same hand he had used for the parry. Even this was not enough: some years later Childs was down on his luck and asked Johnson for a loan. Jack growled, "Get to hell away from me." Summing it up, Johnson said in *Mes Combats,* "I had no pity on him."

In Johnson's world, pity was as rare as innocence or courtesy. At the same time, beyond Jack's self-centered activities, the country as a whole was beginning to afford opportunities almost without limit, even for men of his calling, and even for Negroes. Johnson understood that his best and perhaps only chance for fame and money lay in the boxer's trade. And the money he earned would be worth something: President McKinley had obtained an Act of Congress establishing that Treasury notes would be redeemed in gold. There were those who objected to this, and somewhere, Johnson knew, there was a money

trust, resembling an octopus with tentacles running everywhere in the land. But Johnson's reaction was not indignation at the greed of the money kings; it was an honest
desire to get a share of the national wealth for himself.
There were all sorts of new things that Johnson would like
to buy. For example, there was the motor-propelled vehicle called the automobile, that Charles E. Duryea of
Massachusetts and Elwood Haynes of Indiana had begun
to manufacture in the early nineties, and now an article
of general commerce under numerous competing brands.
This vehicle had appeared among many other fascinating
inventions, for America was not only a nation of financiers,
soldiers, preachers, and college presidents—it was a nation
of tinkerers. This generic trait made it possible in the year
of the Galveston flood for the Patent Office in Washington
to announce it had issued 4,000,000 patents in the past
ten years.

One thing no inventor could supply was a machine to
put the graduate degree of excellence on Johnson as a
fighter. For this he needed contact with human talents;
long afterward, he said that until his career was well
launched, he had been too poor to hire coaches and
trainers, and owed his education as a boxer to the men
he worked for as a sparring mate in the ring. He had one
tutor who gave him an even greater benefit than he received from Walcott. The graduate professor was Joe
Choyinski (pronounced Ko-in-ski) whom he met in a
match that a visiting promoter put on at Galveston. A
Polish Jew, Choyinski was a great fighter, with a reputation based on inexhaustible endurance and the concen-
trated force with which he hit his opponents.

Perhaps the punch that knocked Johnson out in the third round of the Choyinski fight was not the hardest blow ever aimed at him, but without doubt it was the hardest blow that ever landed on him. When he came to, he found himself looking up into the face of Captain Luke Travis of the Texas Rangers.

"You boys are going to the cross-bar hotel," Travis said. The promoter had advertised a fight to the finish, and that was illegal, though he had assured the boxers nothing would be done about it. It was now obvious that he had been too optimistic, but the Rangers had not wished to spoil the sport, and so had delayed arresting the principals until Choyinski had aimed and fired the blow that dropped Johnson as though he had been shot.

In jail, the warden allowed Johnson and Choyinski to box in the courtyard every day, both as exercise and for his own entertainment and that of the prisoners and guards. Choyinski had a generous heart, and he said to Johnson, "A man who can move like you should never have to take a punch. Don't try to block—you're fast enough to get clear out of the way."

So Johnson's style got its final polish in the jailyard, before an assembly of bums, drunks, thieves, and prison guards—not the least knowing audience for this sort of thing. The records show that Choyinski's instructions lasted three weeks; then the informal justice of the time revealed itself in the person of a judicial officer who came to the prison, watched Johnson and Choyinski box two rounds, expelled a stream of tobacco-stimulated spittle, and said, "You can turn them boys loose."

Johnson realized that a state in which the organized

commercial practice of his profession could result in imprisonment was not the place to start a serious career; shortly after his release he left Galveston and Texas, and began presenting himself to the world as a man committed to his calling. He started on a series of fights that would end seven years later in winning the championship of the world. During this time he was to lose only one decision, and that by an obvious error in the judging.

From Galveston Johnson crossed the Great American Desert into California, where he won four fights in four months, and found additional work as a sparring partner with Kid Carter, an important boxer in those days. And it was in California that Johnson received his first expert critical notice, when he attracted the attention of Hearst's San Francisco sport-page cartoonist and writer Thomas Aloysius (Tad) Dorgan. This was a great man. For one thing, he enriched the language with the term "hot dog," drawing frankfurter sausages with legs and tails as dachshunds. He further entertained his public with such characters as His Honor Judge Rummy, Silk Hat Harry, Frisco Fanny, and Reno Ruth, and with a cartoon series that has a place in the history of American humor—the sardonic daily scene called "Tad's Indoor Sports." This gifted man was one of the best judges of boxing in America, and his word carried immense weight, much like that of his contemporary William Dean Howells in literature. Because of his authority many fighters courted Dorgan. It was therefore a great day for Johnson when Dorgan drew him aside and said, "Kid, I think you've got what it takes. You're going to beat them all."

With this accolade glowing in his mind, winning fights

and pocketing purses, Johnson arrived in Denver toward the end of 1902. He was separated from Mary, with divorce soon to come. Meanwhile, another woman attracted him, and there followed a passage in his life that left him sick with chagrin and deep in melancholy.

The trouble began in Denver when Johnson met a Negro girl from Philadelphia named Clara Kerr. He fell in love with Clara, and persuaded her to move into his apartment. Clara had no loyalty to Johnson; her real friend was a discredited racing trainer named Willie Bryant. Johnson was so infatuated that he granted Clara's request to allow Willie the use of a spare room in the apartment until he got back on his feet.

A week later, Johnson came home to find that Clara and Willie had cleaned out the apartment and disappeared. They had even taken Johnson's clothes. The meanness of it sickened him, and for the following week he was in a state of shock. Then he heard that Clara and Willie were in St. Louis. He went there at once, and waited outside their hotel. That night, Willie and Clara came out chatting and laughing, and stopped when they saw him tall and black under a street lamp. Strangely enough, he was sober and did not attack Bryant with fist or knife. And within a few days, Clara came back to Johnson.

A few months later Clara left him again, and this time Johnson knew it was no good—she would never come back. It was the low point of his life: he told managers and matchmakers he had no more interest in boxing. He drifted east to Pittsburgh, and took lodgings in which he spent hours moping alone. When he went out it was only to drink in dismal saloons where he was not likely to meet a friend. It would seem that Johnson exemplified the man in Duke Ellington's ballad, who didn't get around much any more. One night, as he slouched along the street, he heard someone say, "There goes Jack Johnson. He's all washed up."

This casual judgment by a stranger had a terrifying impact. It brought to Johnson's mind the picture of a failure; and in that era, failure would not be cushioned with a government job or payments of a dole. Johnson decided to pull himself together; and like many an American before and since, he went to New York City for the stimulation of its bracing and impersonal air. He spent a week in Manhattan; and then, challenged by the thought that nobody in the city cared whether he lived or died, Johnson returned to Pittsburgh and the scenes of his deepest depression. This he did in the spirit of a man who has fallen from a horse, and mounts to ride again. Arriving in town with two dollars in his pocket, Johnson lived for several days on crackers and tea, and was reduced to accepting a match offered by a group of butchers, who thought they had a first-class fighter in the champion bruiser of their guild. Taking on such an opponent showed the depth of Johnson's decline; but he had to eat.

The meat-cutter was a neighborhood bully who had won a number of saloon brawls. Johnson faced him on a Sunday afternoon in a warehouse crowded with butchers, most of them as burly as their champion. So hungry that his legs felt hollow, Johnson feared he lacked strength to last even one round against the dangerous amateur. For this reason, he knocked the fellow unconscious immediately after the starting bell. It happened in a flash: one

moment the partisans saw their man raise his fists and take
the fighting stance of the great ex-champion John L. Sullivan, and the next moment he was on his back, in the
condition of one who had touched a high voltage wire.
Not pausing to discuss matters with the open-mouthed
spectators, Johnson grabbed the purse and hurried to a
restaurant, where he ordered a sizeable steak, a bushel of
German-fried potatoes, and a stein of rye.

With that, Johnson's fortunes began to improve. He
always said his career took its final upward turn when he
left Pittsburgh for California, where he again found work
as a sparring partner. After a few months he fought an
Irishman named George Gardiner, a famous boxer who
had once claimed the light heavyweight championship of
the world. The circumstances of the Gardiner fight gave
dramatic evidence of how Johnson had prospered, for
just as when he beat the Pittsburgh saloon fighter, he was
weak and ill when he entered the ring. But this time his
ailments came from the reverse of poverty: Johnson had
been earning good money, and had started to spend it for
drink. He liked whiskey, any sort of wine but especially
champagne, and beer, which he drank through a straw.
While pursuing his researches in San Francisco, he met
a moth-eaten Britisher who claimed to have seen service
in Her Majesty's Indian Forces, and maintained that there
was no drink to compare with the Rajah's peg.

"Used to drink it in the mess, don't you know," the
man said to Johnson, and then revealed that the peg was
the same as a highball, except that one used brandy for
whiskey and champagne for soda water. Training for
Gardiner on this mixture gave Johnson such a severe

dyspepsia that he had to give up alcohol and live for the
last three days before the match on orange juice and milk.
But he was bigger and faster than Gardiner, and he won
the fight.

Perhaps only those who live by their wits and on piece-
work can understand Johnson's frame of mind as he now
entered the period in his professional career that would
make him a challenger for the championship of the world.
He gloried in his earning power as the fees grew to five
hundred dollars a match, then to a thousand and beyond.
These dollars had about seven times the purchasing power
of the anemic thing we know today; and Johnson paid no
attention to local tax laws, keeping so much on the move
that his personal property—good suits, diamond rings, and
English luggage—could never be assessed for taxes anyhow. The Federal income tax that was to be so trouble-
some to boxer Joe Louis and to millions of other Americans lay in the future. Johnson lived in a way that sporting
people called "come day, go day." He carried his money
in the yellow gold Treasury notes, gave no thought to bank
accounts or investments, and acted as though he had
accepted an invitation to be guest of honor at a party
that would never end.

During this period Johnson hoped to make a side income from an activity that appeared to be less onerous
and dangerous than boxing— performing on the vaudeville
stage. He offered as qualifications a broad smile illuminated with numerous gold fillings, a sense of rhythm that
made it possible for him to do a dance routine, the ability
to play the harmonica and the double-bass or bull fiddle,
and the gift of improvised chatter that had been his since

boyhood. At this time, none of the vaudeville bookers saw it Johnson's way. They were pallid little men, never separated from reeking cigars, and when they watched Johnson demonstrate what he thought his act should be, they invariably said, "No good." But later, when Johnson became one of the greatest vaudeville attractions of the age, the only added element in his act was the championship. Johnson expressed no bitterness about the change in the bookers' estimates of his drawing power. He knew that theatrical engagements came with the heavyweight crown. At that, he was the best entertainer from the ranks of fighters until the appearance of Maxie Rosenbloom, who developed into a satisfactory nightclub comedian after he left the ring .

With or without theatrical fees, Johnson had a source of income that seldom failed: the mathematical instinct of a successful gambler. Some authorities believe that a public understanding of the odds would cause all gambling houses to close for lack of business. But no such calamity descended on the crap tables that Johnson patronized, and he rejoiced at the endless supply of players who believed they could influence the fall of dice by shouts, grimaces, and contortions. As Johnson calmly took the bets of optimistic shooters, he displayed no resemblance whatsoever to the traditional dice-crazy Negro, praying to the bones. *Never do business except at a profit* was Johnson's motto.

In *Mes Combats,* Johnson recorded that his opponents for four years after the Gardiner fight in 1902 were all "men of color." He would meet Black Bill, for example, then Sandy Ferguson; now he would fight Joe Jeannette, and now Sam McVey—these black men formed what almost amounted to a separate company of boxers, and the newspapers began to talk about the color line. A prize fight between a white and a black man might well carry the symbolism of racial war. It was not a good thing; if the Negro lost, it could be taken by white people to mean that white superiority extended even to strength, and speed of movement. This provided material for resentment among colored people, and led them to maintain that a Negro defeated by a white boxer had not dared to show his full ability. But when a Negro beat a white boxer, the loser's racial partisans could question the wisdom of trying to equal a black man in brute power, when he stood closer to the savage, and even to the animal, than any white. These sentiments dominated the emotions of many whites and Negroes not only in the United States, but throughout the world. To be sure, millions of people of all shades did not care what any given pair of boxers did or did not do; but the drama of entering the ring, the blows, and the knockdown stirred many who never saw a professional match, but read about the fighting in the voluminous coverage of the newspapers.

The year 1904 impressed Johnson with its "tranquility"; at least, that was the word he used when recalling it in *Mes Combats*. He faced Denver Ed Martin, Sam McVey, the unfortunate Frank Childs, and other Negro fighters, losing to none of them, though on occasion the referee would rule a tie, or announce no decision to get around the law. The critics could see that Johnson's style was nearing perfection. He moved so lightly that he appeared to be made of cork, and his virtuosity gave his performance a look of careless ease, like that later achieved by the dancers Ray Bolger and Fred Astaire. Johnson analyzed his style when he said, "My attack is to force the other man to lead—then I counter."

He paid penalties for making it look so easy. To begin with, some fight patrons questioned his courage. These were the learned men of the barroom and the sport page, perhaps as scientific as any other anthropologists, who said that not only Johnson, but colored fighters as a class, did not like to be hit in the stomach. The powerful Sam Langford answered this reasonably enough by saying, "Nobody *likes* to be hit in the stomach." But the crowds never saw Johnson stretched on the canvas, or clutching the ropes to pull himself up after taking a savage blow. Instead, he danced away from danger and exchanged witticisms with handlers and seconds, or with onlookers seated near the ring, and often flashed his gold-mounted smile at audience and opponent alike. There was something here other than race that antagonized the scholarly men in the saloons and newspaper sport departments. They suspected that Johnson did not take his business seriously enough. In a way, Johnson's attitude toward his work resembled that of John Barrymore to acting: he could do it superlatively well, but seldom could he resist the temptation to add a touch of clowning.

Optimism flooded the country in that fine year of 1904. President Theodore Roosevelt had promised a square deal to all citizens, whether they represented capital, labor, or the public. But Teddy Roosevelt had no mercy for the trusts that had tied up the nation's assets and driven many a humble man to bankruptcy. Johnson knew that the man-

agers of these trusts were humanoid swine, wearing silk
hats and waistcoats embroidered with dollar marks, as
they lolled with fat cigars in their trotters. He had seen
the creatures in political cartoons that occasionally came
under his eye as he turned to the sport pages, and he was
glad that T. R. was confiscating their money and spreading
it around. He noticed one good result in the rising box
office receipts that continually lifted his income.

Such prosperity enabled Johnson to buy his first car,
a little more than a year after the first automobile ran
across the United States.* At this time, Johnson, of all
Americans, perhaps got most enjoyment from the new
sensation of motoring, which he took as a royal progress
made splendid by danger and speed. His perfect reflexes
made it easy for him to run in and out of tight places with
the same cool manner as his contemporary, the sportsman
and road-racer Foxhall Keene. Speed laws and motorized
police took the dust of such drivers in the early years of
the century; and in Johnson's opinion, they never caught
up. It is therefore impossible to estimate how many times
he was flagged by the law. He appeared in court on traffic
charges at least twenty times; and six bad accidents
formed a sinister pattern in his life.

Johnson could not believe that anything so glorious as
an automobile could ever do harm. Yet in this connection
he had an experience that made a deep impression on his
mind. It occurred at a California carnival, where Johnson
visited the tent of a mitt reader, or palmist. To his astonishment, the woman identified him as a boxer, going

---

* San Francisco to New York, May 23–August 1, 1903.

on to predict a future that included travel overseas, meeting great personages in foreign lands, and the championship of the world. The seeress then took up the subject of automobiles, and warned Johnson to beware of an accident in France, and another in Illinois. Now that it is all over, we must grant that the mitt reader gave an impressive performance, for Johnson did have accidents in France and Illinois, though the lines in his palm should have indicated North Carolina as the state to avoid at all costs. Perhaps the light in the tent was poor.

At any rate, Johnson attracted attention shortly after the palm-reading session by running his car on the sidewalk of Michigan Avenue in Chicago, earning a rebuke from the police, and considerable admiration from the Negroes of the South Side. By this year of 1904, more than eighty thousand black people were living in Chicago, as compared with thirty thousand ten years before. They were flocking from their Southern farms to a city of nearly two million that had quadrupled its population in twenty-five years. One need not ask what the Negroes saw in Chicago. They saw what everyone else saw—a city whose people believed that within their time it would be the greatest in the world. This being the case, Johnson felt that here was where he belonged. And in spite of everything he came back to Chicago in the end.

No thought of his final resting place could have been in Johnson's mind as he drove his new car around town. He had come for a great event, the opening of the Illinois Athletic Club in a splendid building that is still a Michigan Avenue landmark. Johnson contributed to the ceremonies by boxing four rounds with the noted amateur

George Lytton. The son of a wealthy merchant, Lytton at the age of thirty demonstrated a versatility that was typical of Chicago. Though a devout athlete, he also took an interest in music, and founded the orchestra of business and professional men that became famous as the Chicago Businessmen's Symphony. With Lytton leading the double-basses, this group gave the first American performance of Vivaldi's *E Flat Major Violin Concerto*. Lytton showed the importance of music in his life when he bought a cooperative apartment at 1242 Lake Shore Drive, found that the doors were too small for his piano, and took down a section of wall to admit the instrument. It need not be argued that Lytton could play the bull fiddle with more authority than Johnson, but when they met in the ring, he owed his survival without damage to Johnson's sense of fitness and tact. Afterward when reporters crowded around, Jack cried, "I'll back George Lytton against any man in the world!"

The palmist had said there would be travel abroad—and sure enough New York promoters now offered Jack a trip to London, Paris, Brussels, and Berlin, with matches against a series of European opponents. Johnson knocked some of these persons unconscious shortly after they entered the ring. On other occasions, when he had been drinking Rajah's pegs, he found it expedient to stay out of reach and bide his time. But sooner or later in each bout, he showed the London and Continental audiences why Tad Dorgan had said he could beat them all.

From his first day abroad, Johnson gained notoriety as an American—and an American, in contrast to the idlers and globetrotters usually seen, who was master of a trade.

We should enter to Jack's credit that in this role he created respect for his country during the next ten years. No matter how far he might travel, Jack was always part of the American scene.

II
The Bay

In 1905, the bully little Japanese kicked the stuffing out of the Russians at Port Arthur, defeated them again at Mukden, then attacked their fleet off Tsushima Island and sent it to the bottom of the Korean Strait. Followers of the war news in San Francisco saloons told each other that hell was so full of Russians their legs were sticking out the windows. In Washington, Theodore Roosevelt ruled the nation from the White House, while the huge-paunched William Howard Taft occupied a specially reinforced chair as Secretary of War next door in the State, War and Navy Building. Woodrow Wilson was president of Princeton, and James Jackson Jeffries was heavyweight champion of the world.

When in his prime, Jeffries made a formidable opponent for any man in ring, barroom, or alley. Jeffries believed in his own powers, and some people said he had never struck a man with all his force, as that would be fatal. On his part, Johnson was sure he could handle Jeffries under ring rules as easily as he did the other heavyweights. But Johnson steered clear of Jeffries when it came to informal fighting. The story was told that Jack encountered Jeffries in a San Francisco saloon and accused him

of being afraid to meet in the ring. Jeffries challenged
Johnson to fight in a locked room then and there. "What
good *that* gonna do me?" asked Johnson, as he left the
place in a dignified manner. All of Johnson's newspaper
biographers have recorded this incident, which might or
might not indicate that it had happened. But since Johnson himself wrote it down in *Mes Combats,* we may take
it as something close to fact, if not true in all details as
given. Clearly, Johnson was motivated not only by respect
for Jeffries as a saloon fighter, but also by a dislike for
taking on such an opponent without pay.

Jim Jeffries was tough. Let us examine that word. Since
Jeffries' time, it has suffered such abuse as a vogue-word
as to be almost without meaning. For example, when the
news weeklies speak of tough paratroopers, as they invariably do, they raise in the reader's mind the question,
Do you mean as opposed to feeble paratroopers? But
at the time the word was applied to Jeffries, it had a
meaning that was both broad and exact. A tough man's
bone structure was heavier than that of an ordinary person; his muscular integument was thicker, so that it protected his nervous system from shock, and also was more
supple, thus giving him superior case and freedom of
movement. He had a higher threshold of pain than the
average man, and so could take a punch, as the handlers
of prizefighters put it. The completing element of tough-
ness, however, was emotional, and it lay in willingness to
hit or kick another man, or maim him, before he could go
into action. For details, readers may refer to the accounts
of personal combat on the American frontier. And it
should be added that the long fights in western movies

and television shows, though staged by professionals, are not realistic. Experts in saloon and alley fighting teach their pupils that the first blow or kick should be the last.

It may be assumed that all of this was in Johnson's mind when he walked away from Jeffries' personal challenge. But he could have no doubt of his ability to defeat Jeffries in the ring, even at this time when the champion was only thirty years old and at the height of his powers. A New York paper had remarked that Johnson at work had the grace of a dancing master—and he knew he could dance away from Jeffries, in a dance that would end with his partner on the floor. But a locked room was no place for dancing, and Johnson knew that if he killed Jeffries with knife or boot, he would hang.

Drunk or sober, Jeffries played the role of heavyweight champion to perfection; in so doing, he set the style for Jack Dempsey, the last white heavyweight to personify raw power in the ring until the appearance of Rocky Marciano.* When Jeffries was born, the son of an itinerant evangelist, his prospects in the vast opportunity that America put before any decent white boy would be limited only by his intelligence and the amount of education he could acquire. But Jeffries cut his schooling short at the age of fourteen by knocking the teacher down and

* Gene Tunney, who beat Dempsey and retired undefeated, modeled his public personality on the hero of Bernard Shaw's novel about a prizefighter, *Cashel Byron's Profession.* A former champion of the Marine Corps, Tunney was as tough as they came, but had to endure years of abuse from sports writers who resented his intellectual pursuits and his friendship with Shaw and other literary personages such as Professor William Lyon Phelps. Today Tunney is director in several corporations, author of the article on boxing in the *Encyclopaedia Brittannica,* and a member of the Brook Club.

kicking him in the head. This was before the age of psy-
chiatrists, so Jeffries was not turned over to a battery of
them. Instead, the authorities merely threw Jeffries out
and told him not to come back. He was lucky not to draw
a stretch in reform school.

Young Jeffries went to California, took up the boiler-
making trade, and on reaching his full growth turned to
the prize ring. His talent was great and he pounded his
way through all opposition without a defeat. At the age
of twenty-four, and after only twelve professional fights,
he won the championship of the world by knocking out
Bob Fitzsimmons. That was in 1899; five years later
Jeffries was still undefeated, and began telling his friends
he would retire from boxing as soon as he found a suitable
successor. The title would pass by bestowal; no living man
could defeat Jeffries—such was the almost universal belief.
Jack Johnson, of course, was among the few who did not
agree, though he had sound reasons for avoiding un-
scheduled combat with Jeffries. And Jeffries, in turn, had
his reason for not facing Johnson in the ring; he liked to
think he had disposed of all the colored men when he
hammered Hank Griffin and Bob Armstrong to the floor.

Jeffries' granting of the heavyweight championship to
a successor is one of the oddest episodes in the history of
sport. That a boxing championship has symbolic value is
obvious enough; the defeat of the title-holder represents
the killing of a king, and the passing of his crown. But
as Jeffries saw it, the only thing he had to fear was age,
with its minute changes in his body that would decrease
his speed just enough to allow a skillful opponent to seize
the initiative and wear him down. Before that happened,

he would be away on his California farm, or standing in
dignity as the publican in his Los Angeles saloon. He said
that no man had ever knocked him to the floor, and no man
was ever going to. He had his pride. On that resolution,
Jeffries announced early in 1905 that he had fought his
last fight, and that he would now proceed to organize and
referee a tournament to find a worthy successor.

Meanwhile, Johnson continued to perform in his per-
fected negligent manner. The easy, natural style and the
smoothness of Johnson's movements delighted the more
discerning critics, but sometimes failed to please the
crowd. The veteran referee Billy Roche identified the
reason why Johnson so often drew unfavorable comments
from the audience when he remarked, "Jack gave you the
impression of never extending himself to the limit."

There now occurred an unfortunate event that was in
reality something of a disaster. It was in San Francisco on
the night of March 28, 1905, when Jack faced Marvin Hart,
a mediocre heavyweight from Kentucky. The experts
noted that Johnson did not seem to take this opponent
seriously, nor was there any apparent need to, as he
knocked Hart out of the ring in an early round. But Hart
climbed back in, and the referee allowed the bout to
continue. Spectators reported later that Hart made so
little trouble that Johnson might as well have been drinking lemonade under a tree in Golden Gate Park. Great
was the shock and outrage when the referee announced
Hart as the winner. In *Mes Combats,* Johnson recorded
that he used the methods of Sherlock Holmes in finding
the explanation for the odd decision; that is, he eliminated
the impossible and what was left must be the answer:

the referee had taken gamblers' money. At the time, the decision seemed to have little importance even for Johnson; but we shall see that this recorded loss to Hart put back Johnson's chance at the championship by two years.

At the time, the only spectators who protested the robbing of Johnson were those who had bet on him. Many of the onlookers applauded the unfair decision, because they approved of anything that would prevent Jack from achieving success and fame. Most students of Johnson's career believe that the greater part of this resentment came from his openly expressed preference for the company of white women in his leisure hours. It is true that the white women with whom Johnson associated at this time had little or no claim to respectable status in the white community. Nevertheless, that community resented Johnson's seeking out these women and escorting them to such places of public entertainment as would cater to customers who came in racially mixed pairs.

Jack Johnson did not need to appear in public with a woman to excite indignation. He could make people angry by the expression on his face, as well as by the detached manner in which he went about his professional duties. During this period in San Francisco, Johnson often showed his great abilities in provoking wrath; and also, on occasion, these outbursts of public fury could give rise to demonstrations that he was as good at running as he was at hitting. For example, we may cite the conclusion of a bout during which he had obviously failed to extend himself, when a gang of rowdies rushed down the aisle yelling, "Kill that nigger!"

As the leaders climbed under the ropes, Johnson threw

the contents of the ring bucket into the face of one, then crashed it on the head of another. He leaped the ropes on the opposite side of the ring and ran up the aisle at a speed that the reporters estimated to be ten yards per second. They said he demonstrated that he might have earned large sums as a professional runner, had he cared to enter that field. But so far as can be learned, Jack never made the effort involved in running unless his life was in danger. On this occasion, he shot out of the arena like a projectile and darted into a hack, still in his boxing clothes. For the next week he lay low in an Oakland brothel, emerging when friends brought word that the police had forgotten about the incident. The cops took no action against the hoodlums who had chased him from the ring, and nobody in San Francisco, including Johnson, had expected that they would.

Meanwhile, Marvin Hart was acclaimed heavyweight champion of the world, though no one took his appointment to that title seriously, and to this day no work of reference on boxing so lists him. It was Jeffries' doing; resigning his title in February, 1905, he staged a bout between Hart and another uninspired performer named Jack Root. The main attraction was Jeffries himself as referee. At the conclusion of the dull bout, Jeffries raised Hart's hand in the token of victory and called out, "Gentlemen, I present the new champion of the world." Oddly enough, though the experts refused to take Hart seriously, they agreed that a Canadian named Tommy Burns became champion when he defeated Hart in November of 1906. In other words, Burns took a title Hart did not possess in the first place. Though the symbolism of the championship thus went completely awry, there was no doubt about Burns' quality. It is true that he was small for a modern heavyweight champion, standing only five feet seven inches tall, with a top fighting weight of 180 pounds, but he was fast and had great stamina, along with the ability to strike a disintegrating blow. He was christened Noah Brusso, and borrowed the more euphonious name from a jockey when he went into prizefighting after years of toughening at lacrosse. In the two years following his win over Hart, Burns won fourteen fights, defeating the Australian, English, and Irish champions on their home grounds. During this period, Johnson frequently challenged Burns in the press, and was rejected on the grounds of the loss to Marvin Hart. These were bitter days for Johnson, for he saw like a mathematical equation the proposition that with his defense he had nothing to fear from Burns' hard hitting, and his superior size and strength would be too much for Burns—when he could get him in the ring.

Burns liked to boast and depreciate other boxers. When English reporters asked for his opinion of the British champion, Gunner Moir, he said, "The guy is a bum." From Burns' point of view that unflattering term was justifiable when applied to any fighter except Johnson. Just as Johnson knew he could take Burns' measure in a boxing bout, so Burns must have been aware that his possession of the championship would date only to the day on which he faced Johnson in the ring. And so it is that as we look back now, Burns enlists sympathy for his avoidance of Jack Johnson. And Burns arouses sympathy for other qualities than his prudent career management.

He had an admirably direct way of dealing with the rascalities that beset a prizefighter earning a living at his trade. Curious circumstances, for example, surrounded the bout in San Francisco between Burns and the crowd-pleasing fighter known as Philadelphia Jack O'Brien. A few days before the match, certain persons came to Burns' hotel room and suggested that he give up to Philadelphia Jack in the twelfth or thirteenth round, "whichever looked better." According to Burns' account, the visitors forced him to post $1,000 as security that he would throw the fight according to instructions. Many bets were then made on O'Brien, who was the favorite at two to one when the fighters came to the ring at the Pacific Sporting Club.

At this point, the audience saw Burns draw the referee aside for a few brief and low-voiced words. Thereupon the official turned to the crowd and held up his arms for silence.

"Attention, please!" cried the referee. "All bets on O'Brien to win are off. Gentlemen, you are free to make your bets now as you will." Burns then gave O'Brien a beating. And he lost nothing to the schemers: as a business precaution, he had posted the bond in counterfeit money.

Such was the champion, cocky and tough, who stood between Johnson and the first heavyweight crown to be worn by a black man. Leaving racial questions aside, Burns was the sort of champion the sporting public liked, because everything he did, from his bragging in the press to his appearance in the door of a saloon, striding at the head of his followers, was predictable. With Johnson, one never could be sure what he would say or do; and this from a Negro made white people nervous when it did not anger them.

It was felt that if we had to have Negro celebrities, Booker T. Washington was more to the general taste. A former slave who was founder of Tuskegee Institute and the first Negro to get an honorary degree from Harvard, Washington had masterful skill in appealing to the vanity of rich white folks. He also had an excellent literary style and a voice that made him a great orator in a day when speechmaking was a public art. Booker Taliaferro Washington could get them all on the platform with him— William Howard Taft, whom the humble Negroes in the balcony took to be the wealthiest of all, because of his enormous belly; Andrew Carnegie, whose paunch was about the size of a basketball, and discreetly moored under a tweed waistcoat; Woodrow Wilson, who looked like the Lawyer Marks in a touring *Uncle Tom's Cabin* troupe with his gaunt face, jimswinger coat, and bulb-toed shoes. They were all there, the high and mighty, condescending to the poor and low.

Washington could recall that though his days as a slave had been almost totally devoid of leisure, it was after the Civil War, in the coal mines operated by a Yankee, General Lewis Ruffner, that he came closest to being worked to death. But that was far in the past when Washington made his great address at the opening of the Cotton States and International Exposition in Atlanta on September 18, 1895. In this famous speech, he set a pattern that the average Negro followed in his dealings with the average white man until the middle of the twentieth century. Washington generated high emotional pressure in the Atlanta auditorium as he stood with his ample form draped in a Prince Albert coat, and his massive, potato-shaped head thrown back, working his way to the heart of the oration, in which he stated: "As we have proved our loyalty to you in the past, in nursing your children, watching by the sickbed of your mothers and fathers, and often following them with tear-dimmed eyes to their graves, so in the future, in our humble way, we shall stand by you with a devotion that no foreigner can approach, ready to lay down our lives, if need be, in defense of yours, interlacing our industrial, commercial, civil, and religious life with yours in a way that shall make the interests of both races one. In all things that are purely social we can be as separate as the fingers, yet one as the hand in all things essential to mutual progress."

As Washington stretched out his hand, according to the reporter for the *New York World,* a "great wave of sound dashed itself against the walls, and the whole audience was on its feet in a delirium of applause." Washington continued in the same vein to a closing passage about "absolute justice," and a "willing obedience among all classes to the mandates of law." His conclusion was that such law-abiding conduct, coupled with material prosperity, would "bring into our beloved South a new heaven and a new earth." At this, Governor Bullock of Georgia rushed across the platform and seized Booker Washington's hand, and the audience wept, flourishing handkerchiefs and canes while "the fairest women in the South stood up and cheered."

Washington's message to the Negroes was to learn trades and get on in the world by modest and industrious demeanor. One Negro who found that this doctrine led to disappointment was Paul Laurence Dunbar. He was a poet, and a good one. Indeed, he outstripped most of his competitors by drawing approval from no less a personage than William Dean Howells, the Tad Dorgan of literature. Unhappily, Howells rated Dunbar's dialect pieces above his works in literary language. Dunbar did best, said the oracle, "in the limited range of the race . . . the charming accents of the Negro's own version of our English." At this the poet understandably took to the bottle, disgraced himself before audiences at Yale and Northwestern Universities, broke down, entered a sanitarium, and died.

Johnson's heart was not made of such breakable stuff, and the people who recognized his talent did not put a racial rider to the accolade. So Jack remained calm when Booker Washington assured white benefactors that he taught Tuskegee students "It is at the bottom of life we must begin, and not at the top. The opportunity to earn a dollar in a factory just now is worth infinitely more than the opportunity to spend a dollar in an opera-house." Washington told the white folks that the thought of Tuskegee need not call to mind "pictures of what was called an educated Negro, with a high hat, imitation gold eye-glasses, a showy walking-stick, kid gloves, fancy boots, and what not—in a word a man who was determined to live by his wits." And yet, except for the eye-glasses, it would be hard to draw in as few words a more accurate portrait of Jack Johnson.

Waving his gold-headed cane in the face of Booker T. Washington's disapproval, Johnson followed Burns to Australia near the end of the year 1906. He bowled over Bill Lang and Peter Felix, and also had a profitable afternoon at the Sydney race course. This came about as a result of Johnson's receiving word from crooks and gamblers that a race had been fixed. He managed to place $700 through various agents on the prospective winner. Everything worked to perfection, and Johnson took the equivalent of £15,000 from the moaning bookies. At that time Australian bookies were notorious for their malevolence and sharp practice; the racing public hailed Johnson's win as a triumph of justice.

Johnson by now had entrusted the management of his affairs to an experienced white boxing man named Sam Fitzpatrick. As proof of what he could arrange for his principal, the manager booked a fight in Philadelphia with Bob Fitzsimmons, who had been champion of the world from 1897 to 1899. Now in his middle forties, the tall, freckle-faced Fitzsimmons was no match for Johnson, who knocked him out in the second round before a large crowd. Jack told a reporter, "The papers have overrated my knockout of Fitzsimmons. He was much too old."

Johnson had considerably more trouble with Sam Langford, the Negro who might have achieved what Jack did, given better luck, better management, and perhaps a little more of the showman's flair. But Langford needed no favors, for he was a tough one.* At a later date Johnson told the British journalist Maurice Lewis that Langford was the hardest hitter he ever faced, and that he had "shoulders like a black oak door." At the Johnson-Langford fight in Chelsea, Massachusetts, on July 17, 1906, the action was so exciting that the crowd howled continuously for one hour and could be heard three miles

---

* Joe Jeannette said he found Langford a more dangerous opponent than Johnson.

away. At the end of fifteen rounds, Johnson was given the fight for inflicting the greater damage.

In this year, a note of comedy came from John L. Sullivan, the Boston Irishman who had been the last bare-knuckle heavyweight champion. James J. Corbett had defeated Sullivan to become the first of the so-called modern champions, but all boxers owed something to Sullivan for his tremendous personality and gift for publicity. Both naturally and by design, Sullivan made such good newspaper copy that he brought professional boxing from the barge, the back room, and the private athletic club into public arenas where tickets could be sold and fortunes made. The numerous laws against professional fighting hung on until after the First World War; nevertheless, Sullivan had made his calling an accepted thing, because somehow or other, ridiculous though it was in many ways, people felt that he was a great American. The old champion therefore thought that he had boxing's most authoritative voice, and that anything he said about a fighter, or the game in general, must be so. He had a low opinion of Johnson, but not because of race, although he did admit having no respect for Negroes in general. Jack's conduct outside the ring was the reason for Sullivan's criticism. Here Sullivan was on firm ground, for it must be admitted that it is not possible to frame any definition of respectability that would include Jack Johnson. In the matter of competence, however, Sullivan allowed indignation to sway his judgment, and at last he went so far as to say that a protégé of his known as Kid Cutler could "chase Jack Johnson out of the ring."

Johnson said, "Get me that Cutler." Fitzpatrick saw no

reason for this, as it would be like putting a street fiddler in competition with Albert Spalding. "And you'll be fighting for peanuts," Fitzpatrick said. But Jack argued that Sullivan would be in Cutler's corner, which would draw a crowd. "And they better get there early," Johnson added.

Fitzpatrick came to understand what Jack meant when Cutler faced him in the ring at Reading, Pennsylvania, five weeks after the Fitzsimmons fight. Just as Jack predicted, they had a good house, and when Cutler came down the aisle, the manager already had their share of the money stowed in a leather bag, guarded by an off-duty Philadelphia detective. Sullivan took a bow, the Kid stepped into the ring, and Johnson approached him with his usual flat-footed shuffle. Cutler feinted at the head, Johnson made a movement with his left arm as though catching a fly, and the onlookers saw Cutler crumple to the floor. Those in the back rows thought it was a heart attack. The referee counted ten, trainers lifted the unconscious Kid, and Johnson ducked under the ropes with his dressing gown on his arm. Turning, he called to Sullivan, "How do you like that, Cap'n John?"

As Fitzpatrick and Johnson raised steins of champagne in a toast during the first few minutes of January 1, 1907, the question they asked each other was "Will this be our year?" Without doubt it would be a prosperous year, for Johnson was now an international attraction, as well as a sure draw anywhere in his own country, even though Nevada was the only state where there were no legal restrictions on boxing. They had to have the match with Burns; and they were beginning to feel that Burns' holding of the championship was the equivalent of his insisting on possession of property that belonged to Sam Fitz-

patrick and Jack Johnson. They thought it outright dis-
honesty for Burns to swagger around the world, knocking
over the same British and Australian boxers whom Johnson hammered down, and calling himself champion.
Fitzpatrick decided that no matter what it cost, they
would follow Burns until they forced him to fight.

Burns continued talking with such outward boldness
that a few people began to think he might have a chance
to beat Johnson. It was true that Burns had done impressive things. He had disposed of Jem Roche, the Irish
champion, in one minute and 28 seconds, in Dublin, and
what made this even more startling was that he did the
deed on St. Patrick's Day. Before this, he annihilated Bill
Squires, who called himself "the Australian Contender,"
in two minutes and nine seconds. Such performances
compared well with the way Johnson sometimes brought
a fight to a quick end. And it was true that undeniably
expert James J. Corbett, now a friend of Sullivan, had
announced that he thought "Tommy Burns would lick
Jack Johnson if they ever came together."

Some notion that the public was not satisfied with Burns
as a world champion came from Jeffries himself when a
Los Angeles reporter asked him what he thought of
Gunner Jim Moir, the British champion whom Burns was
to meet. Jeffries said, "That fellow Moir is a bum." This
was no more than an echo of Burns' estimate of the
English boxer, and the reporter asked, "Mr. Jeffries, would
you fight Tommy Burns?"

"Nothing doing, I'm out of the game," Jeffries said.

"But the public may insist that you come back and
defend the title."

"The public can go to hell."

"Suppose they say you are afraid?"

"They can still go to hell," said Jeffries.

As we shall see, Jeffries later abandoned this sensible attitude. At the time of the statement, however, he was doing no more than reflect the general doubt that Burns was entitled to hold the championship without meeting the fighters like Johnson, Jeannette, and Langford who were available as challengers. This was not lost on Burns. Thinking of what would now be called his public image, Burns began to say he would meet Johnson in the very near future. But he did not set a specific date. For example, Burns appeared early in 1907 at a press conference in London and said, "I'll take care of Johnson when I return to the United States." In New York, Fitzpatrick said, "I don't think Burns will return until Jack Johnson either retires or dies."

Those sentiments found approval in high quarters. It was known that President Theodore Roosevelt was free from racial prejudice, for he had entertained Booker Washington at the White House; moreover, Roosevelt had seen action in Cuba and knew what the Negro Twenty-Fifth Regiment had endured with honor at El Caney. Although Roosevelt deplored Johnson's rowdy conduct, he thought fair play entitled Jack to a chance at the top of his trade. The President did not make a public announcement to this effect, but it was known that he had given it as a strong personal conviction more than once in talking to friends.

Across the sea, the ruler of Great Britain made no effort to hide his interest in a match between Johnson and Burns. Using a royal prerogative for inaccuracy, he stated that in his opinion Burns was "a Yankee bluffer" (he was a Canadian bluffer) who should be brought to time. History has yet to render its verdict on Edward VII as a statesman, but there can be no doubt that he was a keen sportsman, and one of the best judges of rat terriers who ever lived. Nothing pleased Edward more than seeing the dogs loosed against a barnful of rodents, unless it was presiding over the shoe at a friendly game of chemin-de-fer. The many-sided monarch was also a patron of art, as he showed when he encouraged the taxidermists of Great Britain by having a stuffed bear made into a hat-rack.

Great though the royal interest might be, the repository of final authority on boxing in England was the National Sporting Club, whose members attended wine suppers in evening dress in the dining room, then trooped into a great hall with a fighting ring at its center. Here the best boxers in the country performed before some of the country's most important men, for the club's governors included people like the Earl of Lonsdale, a fine old man who in his day had been an expert driver of the coach-and-four, and a Master of the Quorn in Leicestershire. Some officers of the N.S.C., however, failed to come up to Lonsdale's level in manners and style. For example, there was the president of the club, who distressed Anthony Eden's father, Sir William Eden, by appearing officially in "a black jumper jacket, a diamond stud, a black tie, and a white waistcoat."

Perhaps because of resentment at the ease with which Burns demolished his British and Irish opponents, the managers of the N.S.C. made efforts to get him into the ring with Jack Johnson. The exchange of a number of

letters and cables brought Fitzpatrick to London under
the impression that the Britishers might be ideal promoters
for his man. He also thought there was no color prejudice
in Great Britain. He lost *that* illusion rapidly enough when
the club officials refused to allow Johnson across the door-
way, and made him wait on the sidewalk while Fitzpatrick
heard the N.S.C. terms. They were staggering, but not for
generosity. Five hundred pounds would be the prize to
the winner, and each side was to bear its own expenses.
The meanness of the terms added to Johnson's dislike of
the British, an emotion that was to get him into trouble
later on.

For once Burns and Johnson agreed. They said they
would never fight each other if they could not get a better
offer than that of the N.S.C. And there were those who
thought Burns was pleased to have an excuse to postpone
consideration of Johnson's challenge. At any rate, he gave
Gunner Moir a fearful beating, and maintained to all who
would listen that Johnson would have met the same fate.
But he continued to avoid Fitzpatrick's managerial strat-
agems as neatly as he side-stepped his English and Continental opponents in the ring. Burns believed in getting
while the getting was good—the primary doctrine of success.

It was an excellent time to be successful, especially so
in the United States, where the *Chicago Inter-Ocean* expressed a national optimism when it said, "We Americans
have some things to regret, but how infinitely more we
have to praise and rejoice in! We go forward by looking
up, not looking down. Let us look up and go forward. Let
the Eagle scream!" Those were Johnson's sentiments, for

though he had an ambiguous position in his country's life
—as did any Negro celebrity—he was an American.

Johnson's optimism at this time might equal that of any
editorial writer, but we can see that he failed to take sufficient note of an element in his country's life that he should
have appraised with the closest attention. This sociological
factor was the reform movement that had risen to power
over the years. One sturdy wing of the movement was the
Anti-Saloon League, founded by the political virtuoso
Wayne Bidwell Wheeler in 1893. By 1907, the League had
shown its strength in obtaining hundreds of "local option"
laws across the country forbidding the manufacture and
sale of liquor and beer. Johnson with other sporting and
theatrical people paid little attention to this, since they
seldom appeared in communities where local option had
closed the saloons. They took no stock in Prohibition; nor
did they take seriously the other massive onslaught of
reformers in the Law and Order Leagues, Committees of
Public Decency, and Protective Societies that were spring-
ing up as expressions of indignation at the spectacle of
widespread organized prostitution. Public opinion was behind these activist societies for the suppression of vice;
there was a general feeling that the big cities of this
country needed to be purged by force: laws must be
passed, and culprits sent to jail.

This concerned Johnson as the dust-cloud preceding
the cyclone concerns the farmer who is about to be blown
into the next county. Johnson was a generous patron of
commercialized vice, though he took no money from it.
And his notoriety in his own profession, which was tech-
nically illegal almost everywhere, plus high visibility, the

curse of pigmentation, made him the most vulnerable
object of forcible reform in the United States. Sam Fitzpatrick knew this, though he could never get Johnson to
see it. Right in Chicago—Jack's home city by the time his
pursuit of Burns was under way—a bringer of retribution
was already setting the stage for Johnson's downfall. The
nemesis was a white man named Arthur Burrage Farwell,
who exemplified the dedicated and perhaps obsessed civic
reformer of the time.

It was in 1908 that Farwell assumed the presidency of
the Law and Order League in Hyde Park, a residential
area on Chicago's South Side. Farwell had also been a
supporter of the Illinois Law and Order League, the
parent organization, since its inception three years before.
He had come to Chicago from his native Massachusetts,
and prospered as a shoe manufacturer to such an extent
that he could devote his entire time to the militant reform
movement, through his membership in numerous anti-vice
committees and the Illinois Anti-Saloon League. When not
marshaling private detectives and special state investi-
gators to harass the madams and saloonkeepers of Cook
County, Farwell said he found recreation in "appreciating
nature." Just so did Oliver Cromwell enjoy a quiet stroll
around his country seat before assembling the iron troopers
of the New Model Army.

The Cromwellian spirit of attack which was to mangle
Johnson found perfect expression at about the time he
first compelled Burns to acknowledge him as a challenger.
The incident that sums up the reformer's zeal took place
in Chicago when a certain Rev. Dr. W. O. Shepard of the
Englewood Methodist Episcopal Church received a

brewer's circular by mistake. The minister immediately replied: "Scratch my name off your mailing list. It is a vicious waste of postage. Your products are not 'specially brewed for people like me.' They are brewed for people who fill the poorhouses, jails, and brothels. You can do no business with me." He went on to elaborate this point in several ways and concluded, paraphrasing the famous letter of Benjamin Franklin, "Erase my name from your lists and know that you are my enemy and I am Yours, W. O. Shepard."

Apparently oblivious of the entire reform movement and what it might mean for him, Johnson started out early in 1908 on a thirty-week tour of the Hammerstein vaudeville circuit in the United States and Canada. His act, which lasted about twenty minutes, was altered only in minor details throughout the rest of his life. A third of a century later, he was still doing it: a demonstration of basic movements in boxing, a couple of songs, a dance routine, and a brief performance accompanied by the orchestra on the bass fiddle. Johnson had some talent as an entertainer, and he knew how to handle a crowd; but as we have noted, what interested the audience was his eminence as a heavyweight fighter who was almost certain to become champion. Long after Johnson had won and lost the championship its magic lingered, to gather a crowd before his booth at a dime museum or a rural fair.

Johnson interrupted his profitable appearances on the Hammerstein time to go to England, where he met a gigantic fighter named Ben Taylor. Jack had been drunk for several days before he entered the ring, and his naturally yellowish eyeballs were so inflamed that they looked like two fragments of ruby glass from a cathedral window. Struggling with a hangover, Johnson avoided Taylor's blows but lacked the energy for a sustained counterattack. In the eighth round Taylor became careless, and the thankful Johnson made that fly-catching motion with his left arm. They carried Taylor out, and in his dressing room, Jack sat puffing on a rubbing-table and called for "an egg beaten up in a bucket of stout and champagne" as a restorative.

While Johnson relaxed after the Taylor fight, Fitzpatrick met with men representing Burns. The Canadian had decided the time had at last come to arrange a match with Jack. His reason was simple: the box-office receipts were falling, and he saw the possibility of handsome profits in staging the fight the international sporting public most wanted to see. After all, Burns was a professional, in the game for money. Moreover, his constant boasting that he would beat Johnson in his own good time may have convinced him he could do just that, on the psychological principle of self-suggestion. At any rate, Burns transferred to Johnson his own earlier hesitations, and began making statements about "Jack's yellow streak." His brags sounded like those of Mark Twain's riverboat bullies: "I will bet a few plunks the colored man will not make good!" he cried to the New York World. "I'll fight him and whip him, as sure as my name is Tommy Burns." The fact that his name was Noah Brusso did not strike Burns as an ill omen, nor was he impressed when Fitzpatrick put dignified words into Johnson's mouth, about "settling the question of yellow streaks in the ring—and may the best man win."

1. Jack Johnson early in his career.

2. Johnson defeats Tommy Burns for the heavyweight championship, Sydney, 1908.

3. Stanley Ketchel floors Johnson in their 1909 fight.

4. The signing of the contract for "the Battle of the Century," Hoboken, December 1, 1909. George Little sits at center (with cane), flanked by Johnson and Jeffries. Tex Rickard stands on the left (light suit).

Boasting on either side was beside the point until a financial backer could be found. Not long after the Taylor fight, the man for this responsibility came along. Both Burns and Johnson recognized it as a good thing when their advisers introduced them to the Australian promoter who was known, far and wide, as Huge Deal McIntosh. A former bicycle racer and member of Parliament, and the founder of the British milk-bar industry, Hugh D. McIntosh impressed Johnson by his acuity in buying up all the bunting in New Zealand just prior to the visit of the U. S. Fleet, so that the official welcomers had to pay his price before they could put out suitable flags. McIntosh sat down with Fitzpatrick, and Burns' representative, Billy Neal, and sketched a bold idea for a fight that he predicted would be known as the Battle of the Century. The keenest boxing fans on earth, according to McIntosh, were to be found in Australia, and he knew the spot where a stadium could be erected to hold the great crowd that would come to see the fight. Unrolling a map and jabbing at it with his finger, the promoter cried, "There it is, gentlemen! Rushcutter's Bay, on the outskirts of dear old Sydney."

Next day Burns and Johnson agreed to meet under McIntosh's promotion, and in November of 1908 both fighters with their handlers and managers set out for Australia for preliminary training, and to build up interest in the newspapers; Burns did his part by glowering in pubs and talking about yellow streaks. Johnson was in a hilarious mood most of the time and took part in all sorts of fooling. He engaged in a foot race with a kangaroo and ran the animal to death. He also chased and caught a

rabbit, and captured a greased pig. During these pre-
liminaries McIntosh gained further respect from Johnson
when he talked a lumberman into lending the wood to
construct the arena at Rushcutter's Bay, the timbers to be
returned when the fight was over. "That McIntosh," Johnson said, shaking his head, "he could give two pecks to a
jaybird and beat him to a tick."

Although McIntosh had shown evidence of his bar-
gaining skill by holding Jack's end of the take to $5,000
plus expenses, both Johnson and Fitzpatrick were content,
for their intelligence service brought news that Burns
revealed nothing in training to give them cause for worry.
So far as the public was concerned, the amount of newsprint devoted to Johnson's antics and Burns' truculent
statements convinced many that the fight, scheduled for
the day after Christmas, was an event of cosmic importance. Burns was a slight favorite in the betting, and the
wolf-faced bookies reported "strong Burns support coming
in from the provinces." Burns money continued to pour in
up to the beginning of the fight, in spite of reports in the
papers about the "science" of the "immense black." On
Christmas day, the papers published a statement attributed
to Johnson, but written by Fitzpatrick: "Burns has em-
bedded in his brain the belief that I have a yellow streak,
that I am not game, and that by starting at me with a rush
he will get what they term in America 'my goat.' I am here
to assure the sporting patrons of Australia that nothing
like that will happen. I have not lost heart."

By Christmas night of 1908, the eve of the fight, Burns
and his followers were in a state of optimism, and sat up
late bellowing "Where the River Shannon Flows." As he

frequently did, Johnson behaved sensibly: he turned in early and got a good night's sleep.

Early the following morning the sporting patrons of Australia moved in a solid mass toward Huge Deal McIntosh's stadium, swinging wooden rattles, blowing tin trumpets, and predicting victory for Burns. For once, there was little attention paid to the probable two o'clock winner at Randwick, or to the dog, pony, and trotting races in the metropolitan area. Some of the spectators had traveled from Melbourne and Brisbane, and others had trekked in from the out-back wilderness, or had sailed in small boats down a thousand miles of coastline. Some fell unconscious from liquor before they could enter the stadium, which was surrounded by thousands of touts and loafers, while a battery of Greek, French, and Italian cooks dispensed hot snacks from stands. At ringside sat politicians, dignitaries, and high police officials, with One-Eyed Connolly, the gate crasher, occupying a good seat among the celebrities. Connolly had bought his ticket, but maintained his standing as a thief by paying for it out of the proceeds of a swindle he and a confederate had worked on a Sydney shopkeeper.

Another prominent American in attendance was Jack London, an author whose works are venerated in the Soviet Union to this day. At the time of the fight, John Griffith London was at the top of his fame both as writer and man of action, but was suffering pains in his intellectual gizzard from devouring the entire literary output of both Rudyard Kipling and Karl Marx. Like many other white people, London believed that Jack Johnson should be retired, and as he entered the press row to represent

the *New York Herald,* he hoped to see Johnson take the
first long step toward oblivion.

The bell sounded at 11:15 A.M. before an audience of
above twenty thousand men and two women, whose
names were not put on record. Burns showed courage as
he went against Johnson's perfect defense, was knocked
to the floor by a counterpunch, scrambled up and resumed the attack. This was the first prize fight to be ade-
quately photographed, and the pictures show the champion's wild frustration at his inability to hurt Johnson.

"Who told you I was yellow?" Johnson asked at the
start. Burns answered with cursing and bad words, which
were copiously returned. A romantic British writer stated
that Johnson's answer included such rounded lines as
"You're *white,* Tommy—white as the flag of surrender!"
Nothing so elegant was said, but an authentic and print-
able remark from Johnson after a rush by Burns was,
"You ain't showed me nothin' yet."

From the beginning it was plain that Burns was out-
matched. Yet he was so tough a customer that many believed he would hang on through the scheduled twenty
rounds, and at the start of the twelfth a bookie yelled,
"Even money Burns is there at the finish!" Johnson yelled
back, "A hundred to one he don't black my eye!" In the
fourteenth round Johnson felled Burns for the count of
eight. When Burns struggled to his feet, he was dazed
and defenseless, and the police entered the ring to save
him from injury. Huge Deal McIntosh was referee and
he declared Johnson winner and new champion, but as
soon as Burns got his breath, he began to curse the officers
and shout that he wasn't licked.

Paying no attention to this outcry, Johnson left for his headquarters, where a celebration was already under way. But at the Burns camp they sang no more. And within a week, the ex-champion lost all his $30,000 purse at the Sydney racetracks. Burns never again fought an important fight: in his later years, he turned preacher and described himself as "a paratrooper of the Lord." From the pulpit he stated that in his fighting days he had been "vicious and full of hatred." This was particularly so at the time he fought Johnson, when, as he put it, "Race prejudice was rampant in my mind. The idea of a black man challenging me was beyond enduring. Hatred made me tense. It wasn't Johnson who beat Tommy Burns but Tommy Burns who beat himself."

Such a reasonable attitude toward the outcome of the match was far from Jack London's mind as he hurried off a load of high-proof prose to the *Herald*. With his typewriter mangling metaphors like a combine chewing up wheat, London wrote: "The fight! —There was no fight! No Armenian massacre could compare to the hopeless slaughter that took place in the Sydney Stadium. The fight, if fight it could be called, was like that between a pygmy and a colossus. It has all the seeming of a playful Ethiopian at loggerheads with a small white man—of a grown man cuffing a naughty child—of a monologue by Johnson who made a noise with his fist like a lullaby, tucking Burns into a crib—of a funeral, with Burns for the late deceased, Johnson for the undertaker, grave-digger and sexton, all in one. . . . So far as damage was concerned, Burns never landed a blow. He never fazed the black man. . . . He was a glutton for punishment as he bored in all the time, but a dewdrop had more chance in hell than he with the Giant Ethiopian." Goliath had defeated David, so much was clear; and London had an important suggestion to make as he concluded, "But one thing now remains. Jim Jeffries must emerge from his alfalfa farm and remove the golden smile from Jack Johnson's face. Jeff, it's up to you!"

III
The Desert

Up to the moment Huge Deal McIntosh raised Johnson's glove, Tommy Burns had been champion of the world. Now it appeared to many students of boxing that Johnson's blows to Burns' head and body had indeed taken away his championship, but, instead of earning it for Johnson, had handed it back to James J. Jeffries. This exercise in the rewriting of history foreshadowed the technique George Orwell was later to demonstrate with so much horror in his political novel *1984.* Johnson was to become a non-person—at least, a non-champion—and it was therefore decided that Burns had been only a custodian of the title, rather than a true wearer of the crown. Some of the newspapers began to refer to Jeffries as the "undefeated" rather than the "retired" champion, while others called him simply "the white heavyweight champion of the world."

The racial element in such an interpretation of events was clear, though from the vantage point of the century's sixth decade, it is hard to understand why anyone would grudge a professional bruiser the harvest of his fists. And in justice to all, it should be recorded that Johnson's personality as well as his color was a heavy contributing cause of public unwillingness to give him his due. Some quite reasonable people decided that even if Johnson were white, they would not like him. So it was that many expressions of indignation were heard, shortly after the Burns fight, when Johnson dismissed Fitzpatrick as his manager. Though changes of management were common occurrences in the boxing business, Johnson's act was taken as an evidence of ingratitude and conceit. Jack insisted the parting was amicable, but in the saloons men said to each other that it was just the sort of rotten thing that Johnson would do.

A white boxer having somewhat the same temperament as Johnson was Stanley Ketchel, a rowdy character who forced the public to accept him as he was. Philadelphia Jack O'Brien said Ketchel had "a tumultuously aggressive personality," and as such he always drew a large crowd, though some of its members would be there in hopes of seeing him defeated. In the fall of 1909, Johnson had run out of suitable opponents in the heavyweight class. Accordingly he asked his new managers George Little and Sig Hart to approach Ketchel, the middleweight champion of the world. They suggested a fight that would be covered by moving picture cameras, with a supposed fortune to be earned from renting the films. Ketchel agreed, knowing that if he should beat Johnson, the attainted heavyweight championship would suddenly become legitimate again. Bringing his weight up to 170 pounds, the fearless boxer decided to give Johnson a surprise. It was a dangerous idea; and he might have taken warning when on the way to their California camps Johnson drove his 690 Thompson Flyer past Ketchel's white Lozier at 62 miles an hour.

Though aware of Ketchel's quality, Johnson had no notion th t a smaller man could beat him, and most authorities believe he told Ketchel he would refrain from knocking him out, so that the bout would last the scheduled twenty rounds for the benefit of the moving pictures. In any event, Johnson outweighed Ketchel by thirty-five pounds when they took their places in the ring at Colma, California, on October 16, 1909. For eleven rounds Johnson boxed cautiously, jabbing at Ketchel and blocking his blows. In the twelfth round Ketchel struck Johnson with all his force below the left ear. Jack fell to the floor, then leaped up as though he had touched a hot stove and struck Ketchel so savage a blow that it tore off his front teeth at the gums and stretched him senseless. It is assumed that Johnson struck this frightful blow as punishment for violation of previous arrangements. But in the following year George Little gave a different account of the matter. "It was agreed that the thing should go twelve rounds for the pictures," Little said, "and in that round Ketchel was to pretend he was knocked out. They rehearsed the whole thing, and Ketchel said, 'I can't fall naturally, Jack. You'll have to knock me cold.' " In considering this story, it should be borne in mind that Little had quarreled with Johnson when he told it.

Whether or not there were hidden motivations behind the action of the Ketchel fight, it was the high point in ten months of sport page propaganda and public controversy that began when the first champagne corks popped at the press conference after the Burns engagement. Replete with Johnson's food, wine, and cigars, the journalists staggered to their offices to begin the writing of a great debate. If boxing were not a sport at all, but merely a brutal pastime managed by sharpers, as some of these writers proceeded to argue, then perhaps Johnson should be called its greatest exponent; but if the game symbolized something decent, and had elements of courage and skill, then Johnson was not to be recognized. Whichever side of the discussion one took, Johnson remained a challenging public figure, constantly discussed and written about. And now there was even more debate on the sport pages, weighing various arguments about Ketchel's presumed treachery, and the ethics of staging a bout for the cameras. Perhaps all one can add at this date is to observe that the match would not be permitted today.

Johnson's next important bout was held in Victoria, British Columbia, where he won a decision in six rounds over the Irish soldier of fortune Victor McLaglen, who had entered the prize ring when funds ran low. This was the same Victor McLaglen who turned actor and won a Motion Picture Academy Award for his portrayal of Gyppo Nolan in *The Informer*. Thus he became the only winner of an "Oscar" who once had a chance to be world heavyweight champion, a distinction that seems likely to endure.

Two months later in Philadelphia, Johnson took on the local hero, Jack O'Brien, whose real name was Joseph Francis Aloysius Hogan. The match was scheduled for six rounds to no decision, and the experts pronounced it a "farce." But there was something here for those who liked to see graceful movement and expert timing. Known as a scientific boxer, Philadelphia Jack was fast on his feet, and exactly the opponent to give the crowd a chance to see Johnson's defensive specialty, the catching of punches in his gloves in the manner of a shortstop spearing a hot grounder.

Skillful though he was, Philadelphia Jack could hardly be called a dangerous opponent, and the no-decision aspect of the match was unpopular. Some maintained that Johnson was taking advantage of the Pennsylvania law against fights to a finish to avoid the work of wearing O'Brien down and knocking him unconscious. Others believed that somehow or other O'Brien had been influenced not to put Johnson on the floor. What they really wanted to see was an exhibition of Johnson's speed climaxed by Johnson's defeat. As matters stood in the year 1909, with Jack nearing perfection in skill and experience, this was not likely to be seen.

One man who thought he might topple Johnson was an amateur, the celebrated Colonel Anthony J. Drexel Biddle of Philadelphia, professor of mayhem to the United States Marine Corps and author of *The Life of James J. Corbett*. While Jack was carrying on the negligent activities he called training for the O'Brien match, Biddle came to the gymnasium one afternoon and offered to perform as sparring partner. With a wave of his glove, Johnson invited Biddle into the ring, and was startled when the colonel rushed at him with obvious harmful intent. Biddle was after a quick knockout and, had he succeeded, it would have been a matter for extra editions of the newspapers with headlines in the largest type since the sinking of the *U.S.S. Maine*. Johnson merely expostulated, "Now you boy there—don't get yo'self stirred up," until stung by a sharp blow, whereupon he struck Biddle on the head, causing him to take a less belligerent attitude.

Though the colonel had never appeared on a field of battle, it was held in some quarters that Johnson had dishonored the Marine Corps by his manner of refusing to let Biddle knock him down. And a great section of the public was dissatisfied with the professional opponents Johnson encountered after the O'Brien bout, although they included such capable boxers as Tony Ross and Billy Delaney. And then in California Johnson faced Al Kaufman, who was taller, heavier, and had a longer reach; with this equipment, he might have been expected to put Johnson to sleep. In the fight Jack treated Kaufman with open scorn, and easily outpointed him throughout the scheduled ten rounds; but he did not knock him out. Instead, as he left the ring he gave the crowd an impudent grin that did little to increase his popularity. Jack had reached a relationship with the public in which whatever he did was wrong: if he merely kept order in the ring he was lazy, if he damaged his opponents he was a brute. All this emotion, this dissatisfaction with Johnson as a champion—or if not fully recognized champion, as someone who made it absurd to say any other fighter held that rank—this generalized discomfort about Johnson was what Jack London had in mind when he called on Jim Jeffries to come out of retirement. And the desire to see Johnson defeated had now become so intense that it focused attention on Jeffries like the converging of the sun's rays through a burning glass.

It had been observed since Burns' defeat that Jeffries was swollen to a weight of more than three hundred pounds, and it could not be denied that he was thirty-five years old; however, he retained his great strength and

could still break any man's grip with either hand. Jeffries
had the myth-making quality of a real folk hero; people
believed, for example, that he had cured himself of pneumonia by drinking a case of whiskey in two days. It was
widely held that he had a mortal hatred for Johnson, and
bartenders told steady customers that if the fight could be
arranged, Jeffries would "probably kill the Negro." Men
who should have known better had overpowering faith
that Jeffries could get down to ring weight, a matter of
melting some seventy pounds, and after five years of idle-
ness beat an almost perfect fighter who was at the height
of his powers.

Flattered by the general confidence in his strength and
skill, Jeffries nevertheless had doubts as to the wisdom
of returning to the ring. We recall his crisp dismissal of
public opinion when asked if he cared to fight Tommy
Burns. All the same, there was something hypnotic in the
way the sporting public pressed its consensus upon him
by assuming that the match was made. "Proud to shake
the fist that's going to kill Jack Johnson!" a barfly would
say, grabbing Jeffries' huge paw. "When's it going to be,
Jeff?" And hundreds of letters from strangers came into
his California home, the writers telling Jeffries of their
certainty that it was his duty to fight Johnson, and his
destiny to hand him the biggest defeat in the history of
the ring.

Early in 1909, Jeffries decided he must take inventory
of his life and career, look into the business aspects of a
match with Johnson, and decide what to do about it.
He appointed a sporting San Francisco hatter named Sam
Berger as his personal manager, and sent him to hold

confidential talks with George Little and Sig Hart. The
successful concealment of these preliminary negotiations
from the press showed that Johnson, who had been called
crazy over publicity, could keep a close mouth when it
suited him. Hart, Berger, and Little moved discreetly in
and out of Chicago and San Francisco hotels. Jeffries'
truculence at the time of his challenge to a saloon brawl
was forgotten; all concerned knew they were dealing with
a "natural"—a fight that could not fail. Berger put it that
the match would be "as good as a license to print our own
money." A sense of wealth was in the air—the feel of the
U. S. Treasury's gold coins and crisp yellow banknotes.

Roving in the hotel barrooms the reporters sensed the
drama of high contracting parties moving to a deal. Lacking information from the principals, they circulated rumors that Johnson was agreeing to throw the fight to
Jeffries for a large sum. How this money was to be raised
no one seemed to know; they knew still less why Johnson
would bargain away his earning power. Johnson and
Jeffries made a private agreement to fight, though to this
day the exact date on which they came to the decision is
not known. But it can be deduced that Jeffries made a
conditional agreement in the late spring of 1909, and that
the condition was his ability to attain fighting shape without ruining his health. With this question in mind he set
out for the weight-reducing headquarters of the time, the
mineral baths at Carlsbad in northwest Bohemia (now
Czechoslovakia). Here he proposed to consult the medical
staff; he would begin heavy training only if they said it
was safe. And here Jeffries received final proof that the
world took it for granted he would destroy Jack Johnson.

The word came from an august source, the same royal personage who had called Burns a Yankee bluffer.

It happened that Edward VII was a frequent patron of Carlsbad, finding the waters beneficial, and the place convenient for his attention to a number of ladies in the spa's luxurious hotels. Thus it was not surprising that on his first morning in town, Jeffries encountered the king taking his usual walk. Edward VII was identifiable in spite of the dark glasses over his brandied and protuberant eyes, by the familiar gray Homburg, "torpedo" beard, and projecting paunch. The lantern-jawed Jeffries was also a recognizable celebrity because of his great height and bulk, and the king hailed him in his characteristic wheezing and guttural tones.

"Hello there, Jim Jeffries!" said the genial monarch. "Going to fight the blackfellow, eh? Jolly good! I say, it's great luck to meet you. I hear all Americans know about furs. Come along and help me pick out a few."

With that the king seized Jeffries' arm and pulled him into a furrier's shop. Jeffries was strait-laced where women were concerned, and he looked on in disapproval as the fawning proprietor laid out skin after skin, though the king demanded his opinion of each item. At last Edward bought $5,000-worth of silver fox scarves and allowed Jeffries to go. Later in the week the Carlsbad doctors told him he could safely reduce to ring weight within a year. He took the waters, and then traveled back to the United States at a leisurely pace, sending word to Sig Hart early in October that all they needed now was an acceptable promoter and financier. By this time, Johnson was preparing for the Colma fight; and one can understand that

knowing he had Jeffries in the bag, he would take no
chances with Stan Ketchel.

Outside the ring, Johnson continued to cut a fashionable
figure with his dozens of well-tailored suits, his handmade
shoes, and his racing cars. And it was as a man of fashion
in what today is called international café society that
Johnson began the complicated series of relationships that
would lead to the breaking of his career. There was no
getting around it, Johnson had women in his personal en-
tourage, and they were always white, blonde, and not
given to formality of manner. Today they would be called
"models" or "starlets" but they were in fact prostitutes.
Johnson paraded them with ostentation, thus arousing disapproval not only because the racial mix was an irritation
both to white people and conservative Negroes, but also
because his flouting of morality stimulated the reformers,
and stirred them to action against all producers and con-
sumers of liquor, gambling, and prostitution. Johnson
made things bad for everybody, and so was detested not
only in Sunday schools, but among the host of pimps,
whores, gamblers, distillers, brewers, and their customers,
who believed that where business and pleasure were concerned the less said the better.

In the weeks preceding the Ketchel fight, Johnson's
favorite companion was a policeman's daughter from Milwaukee named Belle Schreiber. Belle was so handsome and
accomplished that she had attained what amounted to
stardom as a prostitute—an appointment to the staff of
the Everleigh Club on South Dearborn Street in Chicago.
This resort, a sumptuously furnished four-story mansion,
was the most elaborate and expensive brothel in the world.

Its proprietors were the sisters Minna and Ada Everleigh, who claimed to be renegades from an aristocratic family and catered only to celebrities and men of wealth. This was just Johnson's style: he qualified on either count. Arranging a leave of absence for Belle, he kept her in his troupe until after the Ketchel bout, then traveled with her to New York City, where he became interested in another woman.

The new romantic interest was Etta Terry Duryea, and she, unlike the others, had a respectable station in life. Born twenty-eight years before in Hempstead, Long Island, and brought up in Brooklyn, Etta had been divorced from Clarence C. Duryea, an Eastern racing man. Tall and willowy, with a fair complexion and abundant blonde hair, Mrs. Duryea continued to attend the races after her divorce and met Jack Johnson one afternoon at the Coney Island track. They became friends. Soon they were inseparable, and Jack began to introduce Etta as his wife. But for some time after Jack began referring to Etta as "Mrs. Johnson" they were still living in an illegal union. Johnson continued to associate with Belle Schreiber, and at times took her along on his travels as before. In spite of this, Etta continued the relationship and at last legitimized it in marriage on January 18, 1911. Before that, something Johnson held to be of much greater importance took place: Jeffries found a promoter for the big fight.

Jeffries' man Sam Berger had been talking with Tuxedo Ed Graney, who had staged a number of sporting events in California, where the law permitted "exhibition boxing bouts." Tuxedo Ed and his associate Jack Gleason proposed to raise money for a San Francisco stadium, and to supply the gratuities for local officials and the press. Graney and Gleason knew their business, yet failed to convince Jeffries and Berger that they saw the full possibilities of the Johnson-Jeffries fight, which was to be called, like the Burns fight, the Battle of the Century. Jim Jeffries believed that an unusual opportunity called for a unique entrepreneur.

Out of Alaska came the man who was to fill every particular that Jeffries laid down of what a fight promoter should be: his name was George Lewis Rickard. Respected as a gambler who always paid off, "Tex" Rickard traveled first class even when broke. Except for his metropolitan tailoring, he might have passed for the steely-eyed western movie star, William S. Hart; he had acquired that same cold level gaze as a faro dealer in the Klondike. Back in the United States now and looking for a sound proposition, Rickard talked to Jeffries and suggested that the fighters ask promoters to bid for the match. He also interviewed Johnson, giving a journalist the chance to manufacture a tale that he poured out a shower of gold coins to dazzle Johnson into agreement. The truth is that Johnson was far from simple-minded, and needed no tricks to catch his attention when Rickard sat down to talk. Rickard had the backing of Thomas Cole, a rich Minnesota mining engineer with whom he had done business in Alaska, and looked as good to Johnson as he did to Jeffries. Both principals agreed to come to New York to make a final selection among the possible promoters, naming December 1, 1909, as the day of decision.

In holding a meeting to discuss the fight in New York

City, Rickard would be breaking the law. The statute was clear: even the planning of a fight to be held in another state was forbidden anywhere in New York. Rickard wanted the coverage of the metropolitan press, and thought the authorities might overlook the meeting, which was to be held on Broadway at the Albany Hotel. But on the day before the conference, word came that District Attorney William Travers Jerome had ordered his police to break up any meeting at which a prize fight was to be organized or announced. The news did not seem to disturb Rickard, but Tuxedo Ed Graney and Gleason feared the police, as did Johnson and Jeffries. Rickard then solved the difficulty by booking a private dining room at a German hotel across the river in Hoboken. He had already given the newspapermen their gratuities, and all that remained to be done was the ordering of cold meats, sandwiches, whiskey, champagne, and a tub of potato salad. Then, as now, reporters numbered free food and drink among their natural rights.

In Hoboken, Tuxedo Ed protested that Rickard had "horned in on the whole thing." Johnson said that so far as he was concerned, money had always done the talking. Jeffries seemed to be in a bad humor that was not helped by the sight of Gleason's overcoat, a tent-like garment that reached within an inch of the ground. Among others present was the politician Sunny Jim Coffroth of San Francisco, who was said to "control all boxing on the Pacific coast." Someone identified as "a man close to Rickard" passed the word that "Sunny Jim has been taken care of, and Gleason will be in on the deal, but Ed Graney is out in the cold." From their expressions in the news photo-

graphs, this would seem to have been an accurate statement. It also became known that no opposition was
expected from Governor James C. Gillett of California
and San Francisco's Mayor Edward H. McCarthy. In fact,
everything was set. Rickard called for order and one of his
assistants opened the envelopes containing the bids. Apparently to no one's surprise, Sunny Jim pledged the
fighters a purse of $51,000; Tuxedo Ed Graney offered
$81,000; and Rickard's guarantee was $101,000, which he
laid on the table in sight drafts on Thomas Cole's Minneapolis bank. Rickard was declared proprietor and promoter of the Battle of the Century, and as such his first
act was to hand each fighter a bonus of $10,000 for signing
the contracts that his lawyers placed before them. With
this business concluded, the reporters hastened to the
telephones, and then trampled elderly German waiters in
a rush at the buffet tables, which they stripped with practiced voracity.

Out to the United States and the world went the news:
Johnson and Jeffries were going to fight. Not included was
a rumor that in addition to the bonus for each fighter,
Rickard had paid $12,000 to settle a gambling debt in-
curred by Jeffries. Nor did the wire services carry any of
the complicated rumors as to the "actual" deal between
Jeffries and Johnson. Indeed, there was no deal, other
than that Rickard's guarantee should be divided at 60 per
cent for the winner, and 40 per cent for the man who lost.
But as we shall see, the stories of hidden agreements continued to flourish after the Hoboken signing, growing like
jungle vines. But what most mattered now in the public
mind was that the "hopes of the white race," as one news-

paper put it, would be carried "on the worthy shoulders of sturdy Jim Jeffries, undefeated champion of champions."

Students of human absurdity might go far before discovering a richer mine than the periodical files from December, 1909, until July 4 in the following year, when the fight took place. The sporting press and public would seem to have numbered fewer persons of common sense and level heads than the ten righteous men called for by the patriarch to save Sodom and Gomorrah. Along with stories of Jeffries' man-killing punch, and accounts of Johnson's "child-like mind" and "inability to concentrate," there was a pother about who should referee the fight. Johnson and Jeffries had already decided that Rickard would referee, but kept quiet about it so the newspapers could have their fun. It was suggested that an offer be made to the British novelist and historian H. G. Wells, but the idea was abandoned. Then the editor of a New York paper sent a cable asking Dr. (later Sir Arthur) Conan Doyle to consider serving in this capacity. The editor followed his cable with a letter that merits quotation to show the spirit of the time:

NEW YORK, *December 9, 1909.*

> My Dear Sir: I hope you will pardon the liberty I took as a stranger in cabling to you asking if you would act in the championship battle between Jeffries and Johnson. The fact is that when the articles were signed recently your name was suggested for referee, and Tex Rickard, promoter of the fight, was greatly interested, as were many others. I believe it will interest you to know that

the opinion was unanimous that you would do
admirably in the position. In a voting contest several persons sent in your name as their choice.
Believe me among sporting men of the best class
in America you have very strong admirers; your
splendid stories of the ring, and your avowed admiration for the great sport of boxing have made
you thousands of friends.

It was because of this extremely friendly feeling for you in America that I took the liberty of
cabling to you. I thank you for your reply.

It would indeed rejoice the hearts of men in
this country if you were at the ring side when the
great Negro fighter meets the white man Jeffries
for the world's championship.

I am, my dear Sir,

Yours sincerely,

IRVING JEFFERSON LEWIS

Managing Editor *New York Morning Telegraph.*

Disregarding the bumbling last paragraph of this letter
that seemed to be suggesting he accept a free seat rather
than the office of referee, Dr. Doyle gave the idea some
thought. He later wrote in his memoirs, "I was much
inclined to accept this honorable invitation, though my
friends pictured me as winding up a revolver at one ear
and a razor at the other. However, the distance and my
engagements presented a final bar."

With their match settled, each of the fighters proceeded
in his own manner. Jeffries returned to California to continue training and weight reducing under the direction
of James J. Corbett and the famous wrestler Farmer Burns.

There is evidence that he had been secretly training even before his trip to Carlsbad. Be that as it may, he now settled to it under the eyes of the press, and much material got into print about the solidity and strength of his arms and legs, and the aggressiveness of his disposition. Johnson set out on a tour of the European music halls. Etta accompanied him, along with a party of managers, valets, and secretaries; they spent Christmas of 1909 in London. On this expedition, Etta did something to earn her keep; in previous years she had shown talent at Brooklyn amateur theatricals, and she began to appear as part of Johnson's act. Thus they unconsciously tapped a deep vein of public emotion, by bringing to mind the folk tale of beauty and the beast.

It was noticed by the more perceptive sort of onlooker that Etta's face in repose had an expression of sadness. That haunted look was there on the night of December 31, when Jack and his followers drank to "our big year." Johnson, his troupe, and Etta got back to the United States early in February, and on his first day in New York there came an emotional pull from an episode he thought was buried in the past. A friend brought the word: "Jack, I hate to tell you this. They've got Clara in jail, and the charge is murder."

The story was brief but shocking. Clara Kerr, the woman who years before robbed Johnson and sent him into melancholia, had married a man who turned out to be a violent periodic drunkard. During one of these seizures, he attacked Clara and was choking her when she got hold of a pistol and shot him dead. In spite of the apparently mitigating circumstances, the state's attorney thought he

could establish grounds of premeditation, and Clara
needed legal help. Though he seldom got credit for it,
Johnson had a generous side, and he showed it now by
providing Clara with lawyers who successfully pleaded
self-defense. In addition, he advanced money to put Clara
in business as owner of a country hotel. Such gestures are
not made by small men.

Other gestures that Johnson liked to make were not so
admirable. The publicity for the big fight was hardly under
way before he was arrested for speeding in his scarlet
racing car at Twelfth Street and Michigan Avenue in
Chicago. Putting into Johnson's mouth the strange language reporters had invented for him, the *Inter-Ocean*
had him saying, "Stand back, Mr. White Offisah, and let
dem colored peoples hab a look at me." Only Englishmen
attempting to write American slang have approached this
for inaccuracy. The fact was that in the soft accents of
his birthplace Johnson spoke the standard language of
the grade-school-educated American, seasoned with the
jargon of the theater, the prison, and the world of sport—
just as it is spoken by the same type of athletic or theatrical
celebrity today. Unperturbed by the linguistic libel, and
unrepentant after paying a fine, Johnson went to San
Francisco the last week in May to start his training for the
Jeffries fight.

Jack made his San Francisco press headquarters at a
hotel bar, which became the source of fantastic stories
about his training methods and his supposed conspiracies
with Jeffries. And though one set of rumors cancelled the
other, there also were tales of efforts by Jeffries to poison
him and put him out of business altogether. The latter crop

of legends grew from something that took place when Johnson treated a crowd of reporters to cocktails and wine. As the party left the barroom, a Johnson retainer named Frank Sutton fell to the floor, gripped by an evacuant someone had put in his drink. It was surmised that the drug was intended for Johnson, and in the telling the Mickey Finn, as such doses were called, grew into a dangerous poison. In point of fact, it was merely a practical joke, with Sutton as the intended victim; training-camp loafers and errand runners are traditionally the objects of such humor.

Meanwhile, reports from Jeffries' camp at Rowardennan in the northern part of the state had it that "the big fellow" was in a ferocious mood, that he ran fifteen miles a day, and that his sparring partners lived in fear of demolition. This propaganda was handed out by Jim Corbett, who was general manager, chief tactician, and director of psychological warfare for the Jeffries crowd. "Take it from me," he would say to the newspapermen, "the black boy has a yellow streak, and Jeff will bring it out when he gets him into that ring." The racial aspect of these jibes at Johnson reflect how a number of Americans felt at the time the training began—but how many, it is impossible to say. The sport pages were not written for those citizens, white or black, who never gave a thought to boxing and had never heard of Jim Jeffries or Jack Johnson. And it seems reasonable to theorize that such people were in the majority at the start of Rickard's publicity campaign. But it may also be theorized with some degree of conviction that by the time the fight was held, there was nobody in the country who did not know about Jim and Jack. This came about because the training camp dispatches soon got away from the sport departments and out on the front pages, where they unrolled for column after column under headlines about "the White Man" and "the Giant Black." Thus a feeling of racial rivalry began to permeate the air, and people were exposed to it as they took in their newspapers with the milk in the morning, or read the headlines over a fellow passenger's shoulder, coming home on the train.

Some educated Negroes did what they could to deflate the idea that Rickard's boxing show symbolized a struggle of race against race. For example, there was the Rev. Mr. Reverdy C. Ransom of the Bethel African Methodist Church in New York City, who said, "No respectable colored minister in the United States is interested in the pugilistic contest between Johnson and Jeffries, from the standpoint of race. We do not think that Jack Johnson thinks or has ever thought of holding the championship for the 'black race.' Johnson is not trying to win the Negro championship, but to hold and defend his title against all comers, regardless of race or color." Up to a point, Mr. Ransom was right. It was not their color that kept Johnson from having any more fights with Sam Langford and Joe Jeannette. Taking them on again might be more risky for Johnson than meeting Jim Jeffries, but the white boxer *looked* huge and dangerous. And if there were subconscious fears of Jack Johnson in the air, Jeffries appeared to be the answer to the need of a symbolic guardian—a giant-killer who was himself a giant.

Not all Negroes in the United States took Mr. Ransom's position, for many black people liked the idea of a symbolic champion as much as some of the whites found satisfaction in the same idea from the opposite racial point of view. The *Chicago Defender* was the first highly successful crusading newspaper founded by and for Negroes, and it accepted the theme that racial rivalry was implicit in the match between Johnson and Jeffries. Indeed, it hammered this one note as hard as Jeffries was supposed to be pounding his sparring mates. The *Defender* was worthy of attention: the paper had made a fortune for its publisher Robert Sengstacke Abbott, who lived in a mansion, kept a box at the opera, carried a gold-headed cane, and wore a silk hat, long-tailed coat, striped trousers, and spats. Little of this dignity came through in the column of the *Defender*, for Abbott believed in keeping his readers stirred up. His gift for sensationalism almost equaled that of William Randolph Hearst, as he showed in a cartoon on the front page of the *Defender* a few weeks before the fight. The picture had Jack shaking hands with Jeffries in the ring, with the front rows occupied by men exhibiting a sign that read: "JIM CROW DELEGATES." The referee was a figure with the face of Satan, bearded and dressed as Uncle Sam, and labeled "Public Sentiment." He was saying to Jeffries, "We're with you this time—go ahead." Ranged beside Jeffries were three menacing figures labeled "Race Hatred," "Prejudice," and "Negro Persecution." The legend above the cartoon was: "HE WILL HAVE THEM ALL TO BEAT" and below: "The future welfare of his people forms a part of the stake."

In the same issue, the *Defender* noted one result of Johnson's notoriety with a report of nearly identical bills against inter-racial marriages in the current sessions of the legislatures in Wisconsin, Iowa, Kansas, Minnesota, New Jersey, Michigan, and New York. Admitting that the legislative activity was largely because of the publicity about Johnson's association with Etta, the *Defender* commented, "If more of our own men were as considerate of our women as Jack Johnson is, what a great race of people we would be." Johnson had need of such loyal support, but it was true that where he was concerned, the *Defender* would go to fantastic lengths. For example, when Johnson's dog bit a man who thereupon sought damages in court, the *Defender* called it persecution. Altogether, the paper took the Jeffries match as seriously as the most benighted white person in the country: "If Jack Johnson wins this battle," Abbott wrote, "it can be said that he is really the best man on earth."

That was one side of the story on Johnson as he appeared in June, 1910. Had he been a completely disreputable figure at the time, so shrewd a man as Abbott would not have supported him, for the publisher's loyalty was to "the race" as a whole. He balanced Jack's ring achievements and the pride they brought to ordinary Negroes against the disapproval of the educated Negroes and the general trouble he stirred up—and decided for Johnson. One need not look in the *Defender* for evidence of Johnson's rowdy conduct, nor will one find there the complaints of those who said Johnson was tricky in a business deal. This was the grievance of George Little as the Jeffries fight drew near; he claimed that Jack had put Sig Hart in full management of his affairs, leaving Little without return for what he had done in making arrangements with Rickard. "I have a contract!" Little said to the newspapermen. "I am no Sam Fitzpatrick. He can't do this to me." Johnson then let it be known that Little was no longer representing him, and said the complaints and bitterness came from Little's jealousy of Sig Hart. This was too simple an explanation for even so level-headed a sport reporter as John I. Day of the *Chicago Inter-Ocean,* who said, "Few people will be found to exonerate Johnson of the sin of ingratitude." Apparently Johnson did not commit this sin in relation to Sig Hart, who remained in charge of business administration at the San Francisco training quarters.

In that city, Rickard seemed to have found the ideal site for a big professional heavyweight boxing match. Local boosters had called San Francisco the Paris of America, and though it may not have justified the sobriquet on cultural grounds, the city was second to none in greedy hackdrivers, exorbitant hotels, and unspeakable vices advertised and practiced in the resorts of the night-life area known as the Barbary Coast. But even in the Paris of America there were reformers, who made up for their small numbers by earnestness and zeal. The moment the fight was announced they opened a campaign to get it stopped, by letter, telegram, public meetings, and private interview. Governor Gillett felt the heat, and became uneasy. Hoping to please everybody, he announced that so far as he knew, the match was merely a "sparring contest," and he found nothing in the state law to forbid it. Needless to say, all this accomplished was to increase the reformers' fury. Gillett had an exaggerated notion of his own importance and dreamed of Washington. It is therefore understandable that his anguish increased when a Mr. George Rockwell of Cincinnati brought into being "a national organization of businessmen and church people to prevent this outrage." Rockwell printed 1,000,000 postcards with Gillett's address and the message: "STOP THE FIGHT. THIS IS THE 20TH CENTURY." This made the institution of professional boxing itself, and not the color of Johnson's skin, the point of issue. Groaning in his mansion at Sacramento, Gillett cursed the day Tex Rickard came to California.

What pained Gillett was balm to Rickard, who heartily approved of the reformers, considering them so many unsalaried press agents for the fight. He continued preparations and built a yellow-pine arena to hold 25,000 spectators. This cost $35,000 which must be reckoned in addition to the cash he had already laid out. Rickard thought it worthy of attention, therefore, when he heard that Tuxedo Ed Graney was whining at Sacramento about "being frozen out of a deal in his own territory." Tex believed that his collaboration with Jack Gleason, in addition to hundreds of free tickets to the petty officials of the state and city, and whatever he may have offered Gillett, was plenty for California. It would seem that Graney got nowhere with Gillett, and may have even been repulsed from the great man's door. Nevertheless, though Rickard was not aware of it, Gillett was beginning to cave in. There were signs and portents: one of the most startling was the spectacle of fifty ministers praying before the state capitol that the governor would be moved to stop the fight. Rickard took this as gilt-edged publicity. In those early days of long-distance telephoning, complicated relays were set up so that preachers and clubwomen in the

Middle West could make their protests by voice directly to the governor in California. Rickard merely admired their enterprise—that was the way *he* did things. Then, one morning while he watched the driving of the last nails into the pine stadium, he received a private message that made him for the first time take seriously the thought of treachery in the governor's mansion: Sunny Jim Coffroth was worried. He had reason to be, as Rickard soon found out, for heat from Washington was being felt in Sacramento.

The first hint of trouble had come to Sunny Jim from a spy in the office of the San Francisco Board of Trade. Its president, a respectable San Franciscan named William R. Wheeler, had received a telegram from Congressman William S. Bennett of New York, chairman of the House Committee on Foreign Affairs, stating that the "prospective fight" stood in the way of efforts to secure the Panama-Pacific Exposition of 1915 for San Francisco. This was very bad. While it was true that the Johnson-Jeffries match would bring from fifteen to twenty thousand visitors into town, with greatly increased business for the various institutions catering to the wants of tourists, still the bonanza would continue only for a week at most, whereas the Exposition was counted on for prosperity that would last all summer long. Governor Gillett knew that nothing must be allowed to jeopardize the big money from the Exposition, and after reading Wheeler's message he called for his attorney-general. "Go to San Francisco and tell Rickard to get out of my state," said Gillett. "Tell him to take Johnson and Jeffries with him. What he is planning is a prize fight, and against the law." Rickard received the order in a few hours; though forewarned, he was helpless. This was on the evening of June fifteenth. Next morning the front page of every metropolitan paper in the country carried as its banner headline some variation of: "GILLETT VETOES THE BIG FIGHT." Rickard had the publicity of a lifetime—and no place to cash it.

Jim Jeffries said, "I don't believe it." His counselor Corbett went farther, saying, "Governor Gillett doesn't seem to be the sort of man to let promoters go to all the expense they have and then throw them down." Lord Lonsdale said, "This is a high-handed action and most unsportsmanlike."

The circumstances under which Bennett sent his telegram demonstrated the power of reform: and it showed, moreover, that the central strength of the movement lay in organized Protestantism. A good churchman, Congressman Bennett had gone as a lay delegate to the annual General Assembly of the Presbyterian Church in Atlantic City early in June. The consensus of the ministers and laymen at this highest gathering of Presbyterians was that all citizens and legislators be admonished to consider the evil of prizefighting and stamp it out. It was therefore obvious that, though not officially acting for his fellow Presbyterians, Mr. Bennett was reflecting their conviction when he used his influence to stop the San Francisco fight. Yet in spite of such plain facts, some people wrote to the newspapers saying that the matter was only an affair of "California politics." And John I. Day in the *Inter-Ocean* gave the most fantastic of all the explanations for Gillett's decision by quoting a "dusky fan" who was supposed to have said, "Dat dah white trash fighter, he is a friend of

5. An arrest for speeding in Chicago shortly before Jack began training for the Jeffries fight. George Little on the right.

6. In the ring at Reno.

7. End of the Reno fight.

8. Jack Johnson at the height of his career.

Goveno' Gillett, an' dah Goveno', he done stop dah fight, so Jack can't beat him haid off."

Jack Johnson's comment was, "I don't care where the fight takes place."

Mayor Edward McCarthy of San Francisco was out of town when Gillett's announcement hit the front pages. Now he cut short an Eastern trip and hurried back, pausing between trains in Chicago to say to reporters: "I am running San Francisco. I am taking no orders from Gillett or his attorney-general. You can bet your last dollar the big fight will be pulled off in my town just as advertised." But he quieted down when he got home and heard about the danger of losing the Pan American show. As for James C. Gillett, he was lucky that Sacramento was not the Klondike. However, he had his reward. *The New York Times* editorialized, "Governor Gillett has assumed national stature. He deserves the heartiest praise of all good citizens." This praise was echoed in church and reform circles, but Gillett sank into obscurity and was forgotten.

Those who thought expulsion from California meant cancellation of the fight were disappointed by Rickard's next move. Instead of giving in, he ordered the stadium dismantled and the timbers held in readiness for shipment to another location. Searching for a site within the United States, he called on Governor Denver S. Dickerson of Nevada, a man of broad views, who ruled over a population of only 40,000 people, of whom a negligible number were ministers or women. Nevada was the only state in the union where prizefighting was not forbidden by law. Indeed, the state had few laws about anything, and was altogether a comfortable sort of place, with magnificent

diamond-clear desert nights compensating for the heat of
the days. When Rickard asked permission to hold the fight
in the small but lively city of Reno, the governor had only
one question.

"Just tell me, man to man, it's on the level, Tex," said
Dickerson. When assured that the bout would be honestly
fought, the governor gave his blessing, the promoter
shipped the stadium timbers to Reno, and the boxers
followed their staffs of trainers, advisers, and jesters. It
should be noted that Governor Dickerson was not indulg-
ing in hyperbole when he inquired about the honesty of
the fight. On all sides the tale was told that Johnson had
guaranteed a victory for Jeffries. "You heard nothing but
fake, fix and double cross everywhere," wrote Tad Dorgan.
Partly because of the incessant rumor, Jeffries was a favorite in the betting at ten to seven when the boxers
encamped near Reno. Few people asked why a fix would
be necessary if Jeffries was so powerful he could kill a
man with a blow. And no one tried to explain what advantage there could be for Johnson in such an arrange-
ment. Johnson had in cash a $2,500 loan from Rickard
plus his $10,000 bonus, and if he managed to get his train-
ing expenses entirely on credit, and so had this bank roll
intact to bet on Jeffries—and getting the money down
would be an extremely delicate transaction—the returns
at the quoted odds would be less than $9,000. But the
winner's end of the purse would be $60,600, and if John-
son bet his roll on himself to win, and beat Jeffries, there
would be around $17,000 more. So it was clear that some-
one would have to find a great deal of money to buy
Johnson off. And even so, it would have to be assumed
that Jack had no pride—an assumption not justified by

the facts of his career, which indicated when looked at with sympathy that pride was the power of his life. Robert Abbott of the *Defender* knew Johnson better than those who strained to imagine ways in which the championship fight could be rigged. Yet George Little found respectful listeners throughout the sporting community for a story that when Gillett ordered the fighters out of California Johnson sent word to Jeffries that "the deal was off." Few people asked the simple question, "Why would a deal in California be unacceptable in Nevada?" There is a practical lesson for all propagandists here: Circumstantiality is the heart of rumor.

It should be borne in mind, however, that amid the babble of fixes, frames, and yellow streaks there were men of judgment and discrimination. Governor Dickerson was one of these, and he went to Johnson's camp at The Willows roadhouse four miles outside Reno to have an unbiased look at what was going on. Wearing a wide-brimmed Panama hat, the governor bowed in courtly fashion when presented to Belle Schreiber, and looked on with interest as Johnson boxed with the gigantic Al Kaufman, once an opponent and now a training partner. The newspapers reported the governor remained calm when Jack "drew the claret" in "tapping Kaufman on the beak." The next sparring partner was George Cotton, who "drew the ruby" by cutting Johnson's lip. Jack's return was so rapid that Dickerson did not see the movement of his arm; Cotton's knees gave way and he held himself up by the ropes. Johnson stepped back, Cotton left the ring semi-conscious, and Sig Hart threw a bucket of water over his head to bring him round.

"What happened to him there?" asked Dickerson.

A reporter answered, "Johnson hit him on the jaw with his left and almost put him out."

"Put him out of where?"

"Quit your kidding, Governor," said the reporter. "You know what I mean. He was nearly knocked out."

"Oh, I see," said Dickerson.

"Didn't you ever see a fight before?"

"Lots of 'em, but not like this. The others were with guns, where men sank to their death. In this affair, no one seems to suffer much hurt."

Though disappointed at the lack of fatalities, Governor Dickerson called the reporters together at the conclusion of his visit and announced, "I have never seen a man who can whip Jack Johnson as he stands today, and I am forced to bet on him."

The governor was too sensible to issue such a statement without having first seen Jeffries; but this made no impression on the thousands of bettors throughout the country who were putting their money on "Big Jim." Nor did Dickerson's estimate have any effect on the experts who were now beginning to flock into Reno. It was turned aside, for example, by the elderly and famous trainer and physical culturist William Muldoon, who was later to be New York State Boxing Commissioner and possessed such immense rectitude that he was called "the Old Roman." Muldoon solemnly faced an attentive half-circle of reporters in front of his hotel and said, "The Negro won't fight. I pick Jeffries."

The author Rex Beach qualified as a boxing expert because of the stirring scenes of action in his novels. He had visited the Jeffries camp at Rowardennan, and was one of the first literary celebrities to arrive in Reno after the expulsion from California. It may be that he did not happen to be around Johnson headquarters on the occasions when Jack drew the claret; at any rate, Beach was soon writing to his newspaper syndicate, "I pick Jeffries, because after watching the caveman's work for a month, I can't picture that huge bulk lying on the floor. . . . On the other hand, I can picture Johnson, dazed and bewildered. The difference is in both breeding and education. Jeffries realizes his responsibility all the time. When Johnson steps into the ring with him, his bubbling confidence will bubble away."

Equally sure of the outcome was Jack London, who had reason to feel that the fight was the result of his influence. Shortly after Beach's arrival, London got into town accompanied by two tramps called Watertank Willie and Seattle Sam. The author's face was swollen with bruises he had sustained in a fight with a bartender at Ogden, Utah. London at once began to load the wires with copy about as penetrating as that of Rex Beach, and generally to take himself with the intense seriousness that seems to overcome literary men in the aura of importance and significance surrounding a heavyweight championship fight.

London's first dispatch had hardly cleared the wires before John L. Sullivan arrived on the scene. He was there on Rickard's invitation as the elder statesman of boxing, and also under contract to report the fight for *The New York Times*. Sullivan had not touched liquor for five years; he had grown immensely fat, and wore a little gray cap that made him look like Tweedledum or his twin as he waddled from the train down the main street of Reno. Sullivan's first statement was, "It looks like a frame-up."

When Sullivan's remark reached Jeffries' training quarters at a roadhouse called Moana Springs, on the Truckee River, he was so annoyed that he cried, "That big stiff better not come here or I'll turn the fire hose on him! I always hated a knocker!" Though neither Beach nor London could imagine a Jeffries defeat, the atmosphere of his camp was unhappy. The staff had grown: the Olympic trainer Mike Murphy had joined as physical director, while Eddie Leonard ("the Minstrel Man") and Walter C. Kelly were in attendance as entertainers. In time to come, Kelly was to be the uncle of Princess Grace of Monaco, but at the moment he was known for a vaudeville act called "The Virginia Judge," which drew its humor from the supposed combination of craftiness and stupidity displayed by Negroes before the bar of justice. Side by side with Eddie Leonard, Kelly could put on a show that would fill a Broadway theater, but at the Jeffries camp the comedians worked in vain. Jim was in such a bad mood that not even the administering of a Mickey Finn to one of the camp servants could bring a smile to his drawn face. Even the wonders of nature failed to divert him: he remained morose at the sight of Halley's Comet sparkling across the Nevada skies. "I told you not to wake me up to see no comet!" Jeffries cried. "Who cares about comets? I want my sleep!"

A contemporary cartoon in the *Chicago Daily News* makes it easy to understand Jeffries' anxiety and nervous tension. The picture shows a globe with Rickard's stadium at its center, under the legend: "RENO—HUB OF THE UNIVERSE." This was by no means a fantastic notion, for the promoters' office over the Palace gambling parlors had been filling ticket orders from England, Scotland,

Brazil, Burma, India, China, Canada, Cuba, and the Philippine Islands. Jeffries was used to being a center of attention, but nothing like this had ever happened in the history of sport. And he had no way of making Johnson share the pressure; Jack London had spoken truly in saying the attack was up to him. Jeffries must force the pace—and Johnson was an admitted master of defense. Like a helpless addict, Jeffries began to drug himself with fear of failure. He had the strength to stand up and subdue Johnson; it was true, he could do it with one blow. Yet the thought would come, and Jeffries could not make himself shut it out of his mind—*Suppose I can't? Suppose I can't?*

While Jeffries struggled to calm his nerves, Johnson was giving a demonstration of the right way to prepare for a fight. First he put his weapons in order, tuning up his shifts and blows; then he provided a reserve of strength by improving his wind through the obvious course of cutting down on smoking, eating sensibly, and taking no alcohol except wine at dinner. He made sure that his legs were sound by jogging for miles along the desert roads, with trainers and sparring mates for company, and Sig Hart with honored visitors in a crimson Locomobile touring-car bringing up the rear.

The evenings were all relaxation; Johnson liked the desert sunsets, and at the end of a day's work he would stand outside the roadhouse watching the blue sky turn to amethyst and rose. Cool air drifted from the mountains; he would hear the mechanical piano in the taproom strike up "Oh, You Beautiful Doll" and see the glow of oil lamps at the windows. It was time to go inside, get out

the bull fiddle, and cut a few capers. Two volunteer
masters of ceremonies were usually present at these
festivities in the persons of the wine agents Bob Vernon
and Harry Lehr.* As the late afternoon sky began to
deepen, Vernon and Lehr would drive out to The Willows
at the head of a train of automobiles loaded with Eastern
society women and hampers of champagne. Japanese but-
lers accompanied the salesmen and opened many bottles,
deferentially pouring and serving the wine. The fashionable women had not come to Reno for the fight, but to
obtain divorces under the Nevada six weeks' residence
law. Sometimes they caught a glimpse of Belle Schreiber;
on the last day of June, Belle went to San Francisco, and
Etta Duryea came to Reno. Like Belle, she stayed in the
background, and reporters confused the two women, referring to each of them, on occasion, as "Johnson's white
wife."

In spite of the merriment in the taproom at The Willows, Johnson's establishment was an armed camp. He
owned several pistols, keeping one in his pocket and the
others near his bedside. Around the house, after the mechanical piano was stilled and the last car had rolled
away to Reno, a sentry paced beneath the windows. He
was a dependable man named Cal McVey, an oldtime
National League catcher, and he carried a shotgun. We
may ask why these precautions were taken, and if they
were not excessive. Part of the answer lies in Johnson's
sense of fantasy, uncurbed since the days when he claimed
to have been pursued by the nineteen-foot shark. Like

* Lehr was also the social consultant to Mrs. Stuyvesant Fish of New
York City.

everyone else, he was reading the papers with their stories
of fixes and frames and unidentifiable figures lurking in the
background. More practical, however, was the simple fear
of robbery. Some of the ablest thieves in the United States
had come to Reno, or were on their way. For example, the
eminent bank robber Cincinnati Slim was already on the
ground, and the bandit known as the Sundance Kid,
later to be shot to pieces in Latin America, was expected
any day. Also walking the streets of Reno were such
celebrities of terror as Won Let, the hatchet man for the
New York branch of the Hip Sing Tong, who was known
to have dispatched between twenty and thirty Chinamen.
And in the same newspapers that poured out column after
column about the training, the gathering crowds, and the
betting rumors, there were items about Jack's money and
jewelry, such as the story inspired by George Little when
he said Johnson had a $12,000 diamond ring that he had
lent the fighter to "dress up the stage act." Little threatened to bring suit against Johnson to recover the ring. Any
reasonably alert jewel thief, watching the newspapers for
jobs, would underline this item; so it is understandable
why Johnson and Sig Hart took pains to make it well
known that Cal McVey was on duty.

Reno came to a boil in the final week preceding the
Fourth of July. Rickard had the timbers from the San
Francisco arena in town at midnight of June 27; before
dawn, carpenters were working by torchlight; they were
to get premium pay, but lifting and inspiring them even
more than the extra money was the meeting of an emergency, the paving of the way for a great event. Emo-
tionally speaking, for the next seven days Reno *was* the

hub of the universe. And the most curious aspect of the
matter is that while this emotion may have been artificial
in its inception, it came back upon Reno as a genuine force.
On the authority of Henry Wales of the *Chicago Tribune*,
thinking it over when he had become a veteran editor, no
event in modern times so permeated the mind of the
world, until Charles Lindbergh's flight from Long Island
to Paris seventeen years later. And no event, said Wales,
had attracted so many reporters; by his count more than
three hundred were at work in Reno by the end of June.
At the time, newspaper pages were broad and deep, and
in small type except for headlines. Reporters therefore
had to write long stories, and those at Reno made their
editors happy by sending out around one million words
a day—the equivalent in text of twenty-five novels the size
of Booth Tarkington's popular romance, *Monsieur Beau-
caire*. What this coverage would have amounted to with
radio and television added is beyond estimate; but it
seems reasonable to theorize that it lost no penetration,
and most probably gained in impact, by being confined
to one medium.

That final week in Reno may have been the last stand
of uninhabited American masculinity; undoubtedly it was
the last great convention of men who carried the title of
"sport." In this connection, the term did not mean a
freak of nature; it meant a man who was an amateur or
semi-professional gambler and therefore a student of form
and odds; and, more generally, a man of wide and easy
views, tolerant, willing to live and let live; most probably
something of a dandy according to his means and background; a Corinthian, a blood. In his highest form he

could be called a sportsman. At the time of the Reno fight, the finest sportsman even heard of was the man whose fast automobile driving had impressed Johnson: the polo player, foxhunter, gentleman jockey and amateur pugilist Foxhall Keene. In fiction, the type was idealized in Richard Harding Davis' idler and clubman Van Bibber. But the ordinary sport of the big cities and his brother of the small towns could be anybody from a barber in Kokomo to Payne Whitney of New York, who booked four private cars to take a party of "Wall Street men" to Reno; the sport could be a tobacconist in Petoskey, or he could be the old Yale halfback Tom Shevlin, who arrived in Reno wearing a dove-gray waistcoat and straw hat with a club ribbon, and took Johnson for a run in his racing car. The point in common for all sports was that if they could by any imaginable means get free of their women, and put their hands on ticket money, with a stake for drink, wagers, and shelter, then some time toward the end of June they were up and away, and converging on Reno in the Great American Desert.

It is true that the dangerous criminals mentioned above and others like them were also in the movement toward Reno, along with hundreds of minor crooks—monte-throwers, lush workers, and pickpockets. We shall see what reception Governor Dickerson prepared for them. And it must be admitted that the tone of the Reno gathering was lowered by a detachment of hobos and bums that passed through Chicago during the second week in June, heading for the big fight, and urged on by the police. When they all came together in Reno, it would be every man for himself.

There the visitors of whatever degree found a city of a little more than ten thousand, trying to take care of some twenty thousand visitors. Not even a pool table could be rented for sleeping purposes, and every private house that accepted paying guests was full to overflowing. Hundreds of the sports, to be sure, had come in special trains and lived in the Pullman cars lined up on the spur tracks of the Southern Pacific at a junction point three miles south of town. Other hundreds arrived in honking, dusty automobiles carrying signs that read: "RENO OR BUST!" and slept in these vehicles. Some slept on the floors of saloons, and others by all accounts did not sleep at all. For their accommodation, the gambling houses employed croupiers in shifts so that the blackjack layouts, roulette wheels, and bird-cages in which dice were mechanically thrown kept going night and day. In these places, men crowded four deep around the tables. The proprietors expected them to bet substantial money; as the *Chicago Daily News* put it, "the two-bit man is not wanted in Reno today." Col. Horatio Byrne stated that "You will see the solidest type of man at the ringside. Nowadays the cheap man can't afford to patronize the pugilistic game with any ostentation. It takes money to see a big fight right." A sport would have to spend at least three hundred dollars for transportation to and from San Francisco, and for food and incidentals, sleeping in the Pullman car. Most of the sports brought more: Tom Corbett, who called himself official bookie for the match, said that "Three million dollars will change hands on the outcome of this fight." Bearing in mind that his brother Jim was in charge of the Jeffries camp, it is interesting to note that he added, "I will be at the ringside and will make a book on the fight as it progresses, as there will be something doing every round. Should Jack score often in the early rounds with those uppercuts, it will make his backers hopeful, and my clerks will have their hands full handling that money."

Men who would have been glad to accept those ringside wagers could be found in every large city. Covering the periphery of the story in Chicago, reporters telephoned news of the local betting activity to their city editors every hour from the hotels and saloons, recording a few days before the fight that a Jeffries backer had put down $1,000 against $250 at the Palmer House; at the Congress, the senior bartender held a customer's bet of $400 to $100 on Jeffries in the cash register; at the new and fashionable Blackstone, a guest betting on Jeffries laid $900 to $500, the stakes being deposited in the manager's safe. The bettors who gave such odds on Jeffries, without seeing him in training or having a look at Johnson's workouts, were prime examples of the type of sport who believes what he reads in the newspapers. The boxing experts had been almost unanimous in predicting that Jeffries would win; and bettors who might have doubted the experts had the frame-up rumors to fall back on. It all seemed highly convincing at the time. Still, there was information available for those who had eyes to see: for example, there was John L. Sullivan's interview with Johnson five days before the fight. Johnson said, "Cap'n John, I'm going to win. I'm happy as a kid on Christmas morning." Sullivan then reported he thought the betting should be at even money, a considerable comedown from his assertion that the fight was fixed. And there was nothing secret about the telegram that Johnson sent on the same day to his brother Claude in Chicago. The message came right to the point: "BET YOUR LAST COPPER ON ME." In truth, for perceptive men, the Reno fight was the equivalent of being turned loose in a mint, with permission to take away all one could carry.

Another source of profit in the great gathering at Reno, as we have hinted, was in the robbing of the careless and often drunken sports who were easily identifiable among the crowd of Indians, cowboys, Mexicans, and miners on the streets. There were two elements among the professional thieves at Reno; the better class were the pickpockets, who worked in pairs known as the wire and the screen. The latter screened the victim's eyes with a newspaper, or otherwise distracted his attention, while the wire lifted his purse or watch. Even as a victim, the two-bit man met with scorn: more than one observer reported seeing scores of nickel-plated watches in the gutters of Reno, where thieves had thrown them in disgust on recognizing their lack of value. Pickpockets were respected as skilled craftsmen by the police, and often lived in amity with them in the large cities. In Reno, however, Dickerson held that the state's honor was involved, and ordered all known pickpockets to be chased out of town on recognition or instantly jailed if caught with the goods. The other class of thief, socially inferior to the pickpocket, was the lush roller who followed drinking men and robbed them when they collapsed. He would sometimes help induce this collapse with a blackjack, and was despised by all bartenders, sports, and policemen as a human jackal.

Against these predators, Dickerson placed a strong force
of deputized citizens, together with detectives from New
York, Philadelphia, Chicago, Denver, and San Francisco,
a detachment of Nevada State Rangers, and a patrol of
Arizona Rangers, headed by their celebrated commander,
Captain Cox. Even the bandits and vacationing bank
robbers hesitated to cross Cox's path, for fear he might
go into the dreaded gunfighter's crouch and draw one or
both of the pistols that hung at his belt. But in spite of the
guardians provided by Dickerson and the Reno Chamber
of Commerce, many of the sports had unfortunate ex-
periences, such as being robbed, cheated, sickened by bad
liquor, or given diseases in the brothels. What it added up
to was proof that there was then, as there is today, a
flourishing underworld beneath the realm of public entertainment.

The majority of the visitors, of course, knew their way
about, and understood that losing money in gambling
houses was entertainment rather than speculation. An
example of a sport who would be hard to swindle was
Colonel Abe Slupsky, a St. Louis politician who arrived
in his home city after the fight with $3,000 in yellowbacks
under porous plaster on his chest. "It was the only way to
carry money in Reno," said the colonel. "I would have
stuck it on my back except there wasn't anybody I could
trust to do it for me. The night before the fight, I kicked
away twenty empty pocketbooks on the plank walks. The
dips would take out the money and throw them away. The
streets were full of them." Colonel Slupsky also reported
seeing the gutters lined with tin watches discarded by
thieves.

As the time before the fight grew shorter, there came another indication that betting on Jeffries would be throwing money away, and now it was William Muldoon who uttered the caveat. He visited the camp at Moana Springs, and returned to the center of town to announce that "Jeffries' judgment of distance and timing is not what it should be. He will take punishment." And finally, those who were skeptical about Jeffries saw their doubts expressed on July 1 by a cartoon on the front page of the *Chicago Daily News.* The picture showed Johnson in ring clothes strumming on a bass fiddle that was labeled "Jeff." The caption: "Hush, hush, don' yo' talk so loud!"

By now Johnson was in a state of euphoria. He did indeed strum on the big fiddle, furnishing a rhythmical background for "I've Got Rings on My Fingers," "By the Light of the Silvery Moon," and "I Love My Wife, but Oh, You Kid." He clowned for the reporters, and obliged them by falling in with the traditional vein of melon-devouring, chicken-stealing humor that was regarded as appropriate to his color.

"No stolen chicken ever passes the portals of my face," Johnson would say, pointing to his gold-filled teeth. "Chickens see the gleam in my eye and keep out of my way. Chicken and corn fritters are affinities. They are meant for each other and both are meant for me."

Such jocosities leant credence to the rumors, now rising to their climax, that Johnson did not take the fight seriously; and in some quarters the comedy was interpreted as meaning that Johnson had gorged himself out of shape to insure victory for Jeffries. A newspaper writer named W. P. McCloughlin went farther. First he posed the question, "Is Johnson a typical example of his race in the lack of that intangible 'something' that we call 'heart?'" McCloughlin thought Johnson needed an intangible something, for he had "observed closely Jack's alleged 'impenetrable guard'" and could not "see any reason why it is so designated." However, in "James Jeffries, the hope of the white race," he saw "a gradually growing sullen ferocity." It might be supposed that Johnson was in danger if one also believed that this ferocity had at its service the most powerful physique in America. Indeed, the study of Jeffries' body in the training ring had inspired many a burst of purple writing, and the following sentence in a dispatch to the *Inter-Ocean* was regarded as worthy of Oscar Wilde: "Under his skin of bronze the muscles rippled like the placid surface of a body of water touched by a gentle breeze."

When Jeffries read this passage, he said it made him sick. Indeed, the more the writers extolled his size and strength, the deeper grew his melancholia. He was by now so dispirited that when Corbett brought Sullivan out to Moana Springs, Jeffries not only failed to turn the fire hose on him, but shook his hand and said, "I know you didn't mean what you said about me, John." Then he asked for Sullivan's advice as to how he should fight Johnson, and before the old champion could reply went on to remark, "I don't see why I have to be the favorite." Sullivan looked him over carefully and said, "Jim, all I know is God Almighty hates a quitter."

With such emotional excitement about a prize fight in the air, many Americans thought the reform elements in the country were defeated and would never again have

weight in public discussion. It was true that some reformers lost their heads with anger at the sight of the
great ingathering of the sports at Reno. One reform-
minded parson who went off the deep end was the Rev.
Mr. M. P. Boynton, pastor of a Baptist church in Chicago,
who said, "Prizefighting has been driven into the nation's
backyard, that portion of the country that seems to have
to promote and protect the sins of the nation that have
been outlawed everywhere else. There should be some
way by which our nation could recall the charter of a state
that has become a desert and a moral menace. Nevada
has no right to remain a part of our nation, with the powers of a state." As they discounted this overwrought voice,
people had a tendency to forget that of the million postcards printed by Mr. Rockwell of Cincinnati, more than
two hundred thousand had been stamped and sent to
Governor Gillett. And still the ragtime rose to the desert
skies, the bookies in front of the Palace and the Sagebrush
Club shouted their odds through megaphones; and still
the special trains pulled into the Southern Pacific yards
from Boston, New York, Philadelphia, Pittsburgh, Chicago, St. Louis, Kansas City, New Orleans, Omaha, Salt
Lake City, Denver, and San Francisco.

On July 2, a luxurious ten-car train containing a party
of Illinois sports pulled in. Heading the delegation was the
racing man Lou Houseman, who took a turn around the
streets and was waited on in the observation car by a
reporter from the *Chicago Tribune*. After expressing surprise at the large number of drunken men in the streets—
though one wonders what else he expected—Houseman
stated the sport's credo in words that deserve setting down,

so well do they sum up the triumph of hope over experience. "There is ample opportunity for a man to lose a bank roll here," said Houseman, as he lit a cigar. "It can cost a man plenty if he spends his time in the many specially rigged gambling joints that are set as traps for the unwary, but some lucky guys will tear off fortunes by playing in luck, for all gambling games can be beaten."

On the morning of the Fourth, Jack Johnson got up early. For breakfast he ate four lamb cutlets, three scrambled eggs, and several slices of rare steak. Jeffries took only a little fruit, toast, and tea, but each man issued a statement in hearty style. Jeffries' final manifesto was, "When the gloves are knotted on my hands and I stand ready to defend what is really my title, it will be at the request of the public, which forced me out of retirement. I realize full well just what depends on me, and I am not going to disappoint the public. That portion of the white race that has been looking to me to defend its athletic superiority may feel assured that I am fit to do my very best. If Johnson defeats me, I will shake his hand and declare him the greatest fighter the sporting world has ever known." Johnson told the public, "Every fighter on the eve of his fight declares that he hopes the best man wins. I am quite sincere when I say that I do, and if Mr. Jeffries knocks me out or gains a decision over me, I will go into his corner and congratulate him as soon as I am able. My congratulations will not be fake. I mean it. Let me say in conclusion that I believe the meeting between Mr. Jeffries and myself will be a test of strength, skill, and endurance. I plan to gradually beat him down and finally make him take the count. However, should I meet defeat I will have no excuse to offer and will proclaim Mr. Jeffries king of them all."

This mood of statesmanlike tact was missing in the office of the *Chicago Defender,* where Robert S. Abbott pounded his typewriter in a frenzy. "If Johnson is forced to fight Jim Crow Delegations, race prejudice and insane public sentiment," Abbott wrote, "and if he wins in the face of all this, he is truly entitled to a Carnegie Hero Medal." There was no doubt in Abbott's mind as to the outcome of the fight, and he went on, "When the smoke of the battle clears away, and when the din of mingled cheers and groans have [*sic*] died away in the atmosphere, there will be deep mourning throughout the domains of Uncle Sam over Jeffries' inability to return the pugilistic sceptre to the Caucasian race." The pastor of St. Mark's African Methodist Episcopal Church, near Abbott's office, felt no such certainty about the result of the match. To help Johnson win, the minister opened the sanctuary early on Fourth of July morning for a prayer service that continued through the time the men were fighting at Reno. And numerous other Negro congregations all over the country did the same.

One of the most discerning reporters at the center of the nationwide web of excitement, emotion, and prayer was Arthur Ruhl, representing *Collier's* magazine. Sensitive to the surroundings as well as to the fight itself, he wrote: "You must imagine a bright green little oasis, ten or fifteen miles across, set in a sort of dish of bare enclosing mountains—brown mountains with patches of yellow and olive-green and exquisite veils of mauve and amethyst, and at their tops, blazing white in the clear air, patches of

austere snow. In the center of all this a great pine bear-pit
had been raised, glaring white and hot in the blazing
desert sun, and into this at 1:30 o'clock that afternoon
20,000 men were crowded with their eyes fixed on a little
roped square in the center.

"The betting was 10 to 6 on Jeffries and the talk about
1,000 to 1. You couldn't hurt him—Fitzsimmons had landed
enough times to kill an ordinary man in the first few
rounds, and Jeffries had only shaken his head like a bull
and bored in. The Negro might be a clever boxer, but he
had never been up against a real fighter before. He had
a yellow streak, there was nothing to it, and anyway,
'let's hope he kills the coon.'

"That was about the mental atmosphere as Johnson,
wrapped in a dressing gown and smiling his half-puzzled,
rather pleading smile, climbed into the ring," Ruhl reported. Then, accompanied by Corbett and other trainers,
Jim Jeffries strode down the aisle. "I had a seat directly
opposite him," Ruhl continued, "and I can unhesitatingly
state that I have never seen a human being more cal-
culated to strike terror into an opponent's heart than this
scowling brown Colossus as he came through the ropes,
stamped like a bull pawing the ground before his charge,
and, chewing gum rapidly, glared at the black man across
the ring. If looks could have throttled, burned, and torn
to pieces, Mr. Jack Arthur Johnson would have disappeared that minute into a few specks of inanimate dust.
The Negro had his back turned at the moment, and as he
took his corner and his trainer and his seconds, crowding
in front of him, concealed the white man, a sort of hoot,
wolfish and rather terrible, went up from the crowd. 'He

daresen't look at him! *O-o-o!* Don't let him see him! Don't
let him see him!' And when Jeffries pulled off his clothes
with a vicious jerk, and standing erect and throwing out
his chest, jabbed his great arms above his head once or
twice, I don't suppose that one man in a hundred in that
crowd would have given two cents for the Negro's
chances."

Jim Corbett, however, was not looking at his man
Jeffries. He had neglected making a visit to the enemy
camp, depending for information on faulty intelligence of
the gin-and-watermelon school, and, as Corbett now got
his first glimpse of Johnson, a terrible fear assailed him.
He knew condition: Jack had not acquired that flat
stomach leaning against a bar. "Jeff will find his yellow
streak now," Corbett muttered to Farmer Burns. He did
not need to add that if they had been mistaken about that
streak they were in for trouble.

Arthur Ruhl had overestimated the crowd; counting
the 600 journalists and politicians who came in on free
tickets, there were just over sixteen thousand people in
the arena. Rickard had installed curtained boxes for the
women getting divorces who here for the first time con-
stituted a noticeable group of females at a prize fight. He
also posted deputy sheriffs at each entrance to confiscate
the pistols carried by ticket-holders and deposit them in
check rooms. It should be explained that up to World
War I, the cheap, nickel-plated revolver was an article of
general retail commerce, sold for as low as $1.50 in stores,
by mail, and even from the packs of traveling peddlers.
This wide manufacture and distribution of inexpensive
handguns had been made possible by the expiration of

Colt and Smith & Wesson patents after the Civil War, and there were no local laws to impede it. At the time of the Reno fight, many reputable male citizens carried pistols as a matter of course, especially when attending a public ceremony. Knowing this, Rickard divested his customers of handguns, not as an infringement of rights, but because he was going to act as referee and would have to announce the winner. If Johnson won, Rickard thought he would be more comfortable with the members of the audience unable to get at their weapons until referee and principals were out of range.

It seemed that the disarmament policy was a prudent one when the crowd stirred with discontent throughout the introductions from the ring. Students of this affair should bear in mind that many of the spectators were drunk, and others were enduring hangovers, in dreadful heat that was caught and retained in the wooden arena. Well might they shift on the resinous planks as Uncle Billy Jordan, the portly master of ceremonies, called up Sullivan, Corbett, Tommy Burns, Fitzsimmons, Tom Sharkey, Battling Nelson and Abe Attel for perfunctory applause. Jordan endured the blast of heat in a high-crowned derby, watch-chained waistcoat, clawhammer coat, and gates-ajar starched collar. At last the celebrities took their final bows, and Jordan yielded to Rickard, who protected his head from the sun by a hard straw hat, and prepared to referee the Battle of the Century by taking off his coat and revealing a pair of silk suspenders.

Rickard signaled for the opening gong, Jeffries advanced crouching from his corner, and Johnson came to meet him with his characteristic shuffling gait. The action that now began was reported in detail throughout the country almost as rapidly as it would have been by radio and television. The *Kansas City Star,* for example, had engaged Convention Hall for a crowd of 14,000 who heard a blow-by-blow account, telegraphed from the ringside and bellowed by announcers through megaphones. On Long Island a more select audience gathered at the Edgemere Club, where William K. Vanderbilt, Howard Gould, Lawrence Drake and others followed the fight through *The New York Times* bulletin service. The clubmen had an agent in front of the *Times* building who ran to a telephone booth and passed the word as each bulletin was posted. In Chicago, the warden of the county jail installed a special wire so that a description of every blow and counter could be shouted through the cell blocks by a trusty. At the Chicago Colosseum, a great crowd that included many Negroes watched as "illuminated electrical figures nine feet high re-enacted every move and blow on an electrical board." And at Twenty-seventh and State Street in the Black Belt, Manager Robert Motts stood on the stage of the Pekin Theater and read reports on slips of paper brought from a telegrapher in the wings.

The story these various facilities told, though its end was evident from the start, had moments of intense excitement. Jeffries immediately took the fight to Johnson, and Jack worked with extreme caution in avoiding these opening rushes. His face was impassive, and his movements so economical that only an expert and unprejudiced eye could appreciate their smoothness and speed. As for Jeffries, for all his crouching, rushing, and swinging, there was no continuity to his work; yet the crowd cheered him

at the end of the first round. Most of the spectators believed Jeffries was going to pin Johnson in a corner and
beat down his defense by main strength, and that everybody would then go home happy and rich. There was a
comfortable murmur throughout the arena, like that of a
concert audience settling down after preliminary selections
for the main symphonic work.

The second round was much the same, Jeffries trying
to reach Jack by means of a straight left, but doing no
damage. Johnson still looked solemn and thoughtful, with
the expression of one who is listening to sad news, or
attending a funeral. The sports took this as evidence of
fear—and did not know what to think when in the middle
of the next round Johnson suddenly flicked out his left
glove in a jab that brought the crouching Jeffries up
straight as though he had run into the edge of an open
door. Now it was seen that Johnson was smiling, and talking to Jeffries. Corbett heard him say, "Come on now, Mr.
Jeff. Let me see what you got. *Do* something, man. This
is for the cham-*peenship*." There was less rejoicing in the
audience when this third round ended, but they were more
puzzled than alarmed.

In the fourth round, Johnson took the offensive, and
kept the left jab flickering in Jeffries' face. "I can go on like
this all afternoon, Mr. Jeff," said Johnson, and so he did
continue throughout the fifth and sixth rounds. At the
opening of the seventh round, Jack shuffled out with such
deceptive quickness that he was able to land a stupefying
right cross to the jaw before Jeffries' hands were in position. From this point on, anyone who knew about fighting
could see that Jeffries had no chance—except the remote

one of Johnson's leaving himself open to a lucky blow. Boxing wildly, visibly slowing down, Jeffries managed to last the round, and collapsed on his stool with his right eye closing, his face marked and swollen. He endured more pounding in the eighth round, and then tried to take the initiative in the ninth, but he hit only elbows and gloves. To the horror of the crowd, Jeffries had lost his breath by the end of the twelfth round, and was still struggling to get air into his lungs when the bell brought the men out for the thirteenth. By this time, some were yelling, "Stop it! Don't let him be knocked out!"—but Rickard allowed the fight to go on, and Johnson kept smashing away left and right. By the end of the fourteenth round, Jeffries was in such distress that he could barely raise his arms. In the fifteenth, Jack knocked Jeffries half out of the ring; friends pushed him back, Rickard ignoring this violation of the rules, and Johnson chopped him down again with a left to the head. Somehow Jeffries got on his feet, to receive three snapping blows to the face that knocked him back on the floor. Sam Berger threw in a towel to concede defeat, but Rickard did not see it, and counted ten over Jeffries. Then Rickard lifted the fist of Jack Johnson as indisputable heavyweight champion of the world.

IV
Lively Times

At the Pekin Theater, a man holding a slip of paper ran on the stage. Robert Motts took the paper, glanced at it, raised himself on his toes and filled his lungs. With arms extended he bellowed, "Johnson wins!" It seemed as if the roof fell in; then the members of the audience rushed for the street, climbing each other's backs in the doorways. Into State Street they poured to join thousands of other Negroes, who were capering, shouting, and beating on dishpans, while over it all the continuous thundering of extra-large firecrackers sounded like the noise of a great battle. Across the country similar parades were forming, principally in Negro neighborhoods, but sometimes on white territory as well. At this moment, about 3:45 P.M. Reno time, white persons viewing the Negro demonstrations took no action, and some applauded the celebrators, though probably with ironic intent. The trouble would come with darkness when the liquor got to work.

As night came on, frolic turned into riot and riot into civil war, small in scale but deadly in result. Exulting Negroes clashed with frightened or resentful whites in both the North and South, and by morning reports of death and injury had come from towns and cities in

115

Pennsylvania, Maryland, Ohio, Mississippi, Virginia, Missouri, Georgia, Arkansas, and Colorado. There had been a gun battle at Uvaldia, Georgia, leaving three Negroes dead and scores of whites and Negroes wounded. This was the worst rioting of the night, but throughout the country there were eight other deaths that could be charged to the racial friction arising from Johnson's victory and Jeffries' defeat. In Washington, Pennsylvania, a nine-year-old girl was killed by a bullet fired by Negroes into a group of whites. A Negro wounded a conductor on the Iron Mountain Railroad near Little Rock with a revolver shot. Another train conductor was shot near Tallulah, Louisiana. In addition to the shootings, there were hundreds of fights with stones, clubs, and fists involving thousands of combatants. In the New York metropolitan area, Irish hoodlums as well as Negro rowdies welcomed the chance to make trouble. A typical uproar took place in Brooklyn when three Irish toughs heard a Negro named Edward Coleman say to a dog, "Lie down there, Jeffries."

"You have your nerve to call that dog Jeffries," said John Dermody. "Why don't you call it Johnson?"

"Because Johnson is black and this dog is yellow," answered Coleman. Then the fight started, but it was not one-sided, as Coleman had friends nearby.

In Muskogee, Oklahoma, a man who claimed to be a second cousin of John L. Sullivan attacked two Negroes with a knife, but was seized by the police before he could do any damage. Negroes shot up the town of Mounds, Illinois, killing a constable of their own race. In Pittsburgh, Negroes ejected whites from street cars and took over Wylie Avenue until police reserves were called. Negroes and sailors fought in the streets of Norfolk, Virginia, where a detachment of Marines helped restore order. There was rioting in Philadelphia, Baltimore, and Wilmington, resulting in many injuries and hundreds of arrests, and the entire town of Keystone, West Virginia, was in the control of a Negro mob until late in the afternoon of July 5. All told, two white persons and nine Negroes met death, the Negro victims including two killed by their own people.

At Reno, the series of happenings that triggered the rioting had come to a confused end. As Rickard pushed him away from the collapsed form of Jeffries in the ropes, Johnson said to Sig Hart, "I think I'll give one glove to Corbett and one to Jeff." But Corbett hurried Jeffries away without waiting for any gestures from Johnson. Though not gravely damaged, Jeffries looked like the beaten man he was with his closed eye, swollen lips, and fumbling movements. Corbett and Farmer Burns helped him from the ring; then he pulled himself together and stalked away. One has the feeling that Jeffries was entitled to some recognition of his gameness; but his performance had been so poor, and his defeat such a disappointment— and to many, such an unpleasant surprise—that there were no cheers to warm his heart as he left the arena. Nor were there any cheers for Johnson. The spectators filed out, buzzing with gloomy conversation as though they had been witnesses to the legal execution of some popular public figure. Those who came armed picked up their weapons at the check rooms; but the only shot fired in Reno all that afternoon and evening came when a miner accidentally dropped his pistol in a saloon. Wise after the

fact, we might now say that Rickard's disarming of the
spectators was an unnecessary precaution. But the situation facing Rickard held at least enough tension to start
some long-lived rumors, of which the one most generally
believed today has it that Sig Hart hustled Jack out of
the arena to an automobile and drove a fast fifty miles into
the desert to a special train waiting at a lonely stop. The
fact is that the last time Jack fled the scene of a prize fight
had been six years before, in San Francisco. In Reno, he
walked out unmolested and went back to The Willows,
where he put on a blue silk suit and a crimson bow tie.
Etta had seen the fight from one of Rickard's ladies' box
seats; she now changed her costume, putting on a fresh
pongee dress and picture hat, and joined Jack for a ride
through the center of Reno in the back seat of an open
touring car. Johnson appeared to be in no danger and the
crowd was apathetic. It appeared that those who had an
emotional as well as financial investment in Jeffries were
still in shock. Indeed, when Jack's car halted in that crowd
that filled the street in front of the Golden Hotel, many
persons came up and shook his hand. He left Reno at
9:50 P.M. in a special car attached to a train bound for
Chicago. The car was fitted with a buffet, phonograph,
and piano; Jack was happy, and chatted genially with
Hart and others; he was observed to be consuming "his
share of the champagne" but not dead drunk. Over the
desert sped the Johnson car, its lighted windows passing
with a jangle of ragtime and a swirl of dust that settled
under the stars.

Jim Jeffries also was riding in a private car, but heading
for San Francisco. He was attended by his wife, Berger,

Farmer Burns, Corbett, and several reporters. Morose and melancholy, Jeffries took no liquor; surprisingly, he spoke with frankness to the newspapermen. This moment of truth immediately after the fight has significance in connection with the sport page theorizing that appeared the following week. "I could never have whipped Jack Johnson at my best," said Jeffries. "I couldn't have hit him. No, I couldn't have reached him in a thousand years."

Next day Johnson's car, the last one on the train, pulled in at Carlin, Nevada, where he heard the rumor that he had been shot dead the night before during a holdup at The Willows in which the bandits had taken his jewelry and a vast sum in cash. Johnson laughed at this, but he did have with him on the train a fortune in cash and good checks signed by Rickard. Jack's share of the guarantee was $60,600, and he had sold his part of the moving picture rights for $50,000. Jeffries had $40,400 from the guarantee and he too had cashed his moving picture rights in advance for $50,000, a singularly lucky piece of business, as we shall see. And we recall that each man also had a $10,000 additional honorarium from Tex Rickard. Either boxer's reward was far more than had ever been earned up to that time in a single exhibition of any sort of talent, including that of matinee idols and opera stars. One must ask pardon for pointing out again that no Federal income tax applied to this money and the dollars were loaded with a purchasing power that is hard to imagine today.

Though rich, Jack suffered the same hangover that attacks any man, and came to breakfast with an icebag on his head. This was before the wide commercial distribution of the monoaceticacidester of salicylic acid commonly called aspirin, but Johnson, like millions of others, had a dependable headache remedy in Orangeine Powders, a preparation containing a powerful medicine. He also took two ounces of brandy shaken up with a raw egg, sugar, and nutmeg. At this point someone asked if he had been hurt in the fight. "I was never in danger at any time," Jack said. "Jeff wore himself out."

So it went until the train arrived at Ogden, Utah, where an ominous event took place. Seeing Jack at the car window, three hoodlums rushed at the rear entrance of the car. As they reached for the handrails to pull themselves up, a railroad detective on the back platform spat tobacco in the eyes of the first and kicked the second in the face. Local police then took the rowdies away. Johnson paid little attention, but Sig Hart felt a certain anxiety: When pursued in San Francisco, Jack had baited the crowd with what looked like indolent performance; but no one could say he had not fought a good fight in Reno. These ruffians, therefore, were hostile simply because he was Jack Johnson. Perhaps he should not have beaten Jeffries so decisively; perhaps he should have had the forethought to be born with a white skin. Hart shook his head sadly; there might be many things in the future less pleasant than ragtime and champagne. Meanwhile, the only result of the incipient brawl at Ogden was another nationwide rumor that Johnson had been killed. "They shot him on a train going through Utah," the bartenders said, as they polished the cocktail glasses and set them in rows. "Train robbers it was. They took half a million in cash."

There seemed to be no anti-Johnson sentiment when the train rolled into Wyoming and stopped at Cheyenne. At this place a friendly and orderly crowd surrounded the car. Johnson got out, answered questions, bowed politely to the women, and acknowledged the cheers of a number of Negro soldiers from nearby Camp Russel. A Negro woman brought a baby and said she had named him after the champion; Johnson carefully shook his namesake's tiny hand.

Looking over the papers the newsboys put aboard Johnson's car at every stop, Sig Hart saw there had been no serious trouble in Chicago, the place where many elements of violence lay in plain view. For here was Johnson's house at 3344 South Wabash Avenue, kept by his mother and sisters, surrounded by wildly excited people who blocked the traffic all day. Reporters had gathered in the kitchen along with neighbors and family friends. Tina Johnson's hospitality was superb; under her direction, cooks were preparing chicken, pot roast, sauerkraut, sweet potatoes, and spaghetti, and there was plenty to drink. At the news that Johnson had won, Tina said to the journalists, "I'm not surprised, not one little bit. I knew it all the time, because Jack told me so. He will be back day after tomorrow, and tell you all you want to know." Pressed to say more, Tina went on, "Over at the church they were praying, and Jack was fighting—and God heard their prayers." A woman writer on the *Inter-Ocean* added the comment: "This was as near as Mrs. Johnson will ever come to admitting that there is a power in the universe to compare to her son."

Johnson's train came into the vaulted shed at the Dearborn Street station at five minutes past two on July 6. The police were worried because the train was two hours late, and the people waiting for Johnson had become restless. There had been a stampede when a cry went up, "There he is!"—and the crowd rushed at a sturdy, well-dressed colored man who looked remarkably like Johnson. He was Rube Foster, star pitcher on the Negro professional baseball team, the American Giants.*

It was a great day for crowd estimators. There seemed to be one of these experts on each Chicago paper, and their findings varied, some of them counting up to ten thousand people in the crowd. They also varied in their estimates of how many in the gathering were Negroes, but it now seems most likely that two of every three spectators were black. In any event, the Negroes caught the eyes of the reporters, and most of the descriptive matter in the papers next day had to do with their actions.

Johnson's train arrived just as the excitement about Rube Foster died down, and those who had forced their way into the shed sent back a roar of "Here he comes!" Johnson made his appearance wearing a smart Norfolk jacket and beret, and his chryselephantine smile could be seen from every corner of the huge room. As a squad of police slowly made way for Johnson through the crowd,

---

* Andrew Foster was one of the greatest professional players before the time when Negroes were accepted in the major leagues. Pitching an exhibition game for the American Giants, he defeated the Philadelphia Athletics in 1902, and the Giants appropriated for Foster the nickname of the losing pitcher, George (Rube) Waddell. In 1920, Foster was a key figure in starting the National Baseball League, "the most successful and soundest Negro league organization in baseball history," according to the sports historian A. S. Young.

the newspapermen heard some remarkable conversations, which they were quick to put on paper when they got back to their typewriters. For instance, there was the speech of the "dusky patriarch" who held up a small child, saying, "Now watch close dere, honey, 'cause you're goin' to see de greatest cullud man dat ever lived."

When Johnson reached the sidewalk he was met by a band of small Negro girls with red, white, and blue ribbons in their pigtails, waving American flags, and the Eighth Regiment Band, which burst out with "There'll Be a Hot Time in the Old Town Tonight."

The crowd was in a good humor. Such at least was the evidence of incidents like one that caught the eye of a reporter for the *Daily News*: " 'Git out of the way there,' one colored man would yell to another, 'an' make room for the man what showed Jack how to use his fists.' 'Oh, go 'long with you. You never knowed Jack, even. Why, man, me and Jack is old friends. He told me to be here to meet him when he comes home with de bacon. I won money on Jack and I'se goin' to be here to gib him de glad hand. Who yo' think yo' is, anyhow?' And both broke into hearty laughter."

There had been plans for a parade from the station to Johnson's house; but Colonel Leroy T. Steward, chief of the Chicago police, gave orders that it was not to be. Like Sig Hart, he had read the papers, and knew that his city contained the materials for racial conflagration, ready and waiting for a spark. Chicago did have a bloody race riot, but that was nine years later. And Chicago's riot, when it came, represented a clash between Studs Lonigan and Bigger Thomas; Jack Johnson had nothing to do with it.

As Johnson crossed the sidewalk and stepped into an openbacked automobile, a little man darted from the crowd and pressed a paper into his hand. The experienced Johnson refused to close his fingers around the document and it fell to the sidewalk. It was a court summons to answer a suit by George Little for the recovery of the diamond ring he said he had lent Johnson. Nothing came of this, but it began to appear that Little's dislike of Johnson had grown so intense as to disturb his recognition of reality: in announcing the suit about the ring, he added an accusation that Johnson took part in a plot to let Jeffries last through fifteen rounds to make a better show for the moving pictures. Johnson had been so angry at Little in Reno that he had threatened to shoot him on sight; now he forgot the bitterness as he brushed the paper into the street with the sole of his hand-made shoe and went on to his triumph.

It made no difference what Chief Steward said: scores of automobiles fell in behind Johnson's car as it turned south on Wabash Avenue, and nearly all the Negroes who had waited in the railroad station came hurrying after, running, walking to catch breath, then running again. At Johnson's house, the crowd estimators had more work awaiting them; some said there were 2,000 people in the street, while others did whatever crowd estimators do, and got results as high as fifteen thousand, counting a delegation of Negro Knights of Pythias in full dress uniforms of black and gold. Whatever its numerical total may have been, the crowd had gathered in such a dense mass that Johnson could not get out of his car until police cleared a path to the house. One paper reported that "the blue coats used their clubs freely."

No club landed on Johnson's head, to be sure, and when he was finally wedged through the front door, his mother and sisters received him with hilarity and joy. Etta was not present, having gone to a Loop hotel after the excitement at the station died down. When asked what he planned to do, Johnson said, "I have enough money to last until next week. I plan to sleep some, eat a pile of good eatables, and drive my racer."

"How about getting stopped for speeding, Jack?" one of the reporters asked.

"You know, sometimes you just can't help lettin' her out," Johnson said, "and then you can't tell just how fast you're going." There was no suggestion that Jack might get some idea of how fast the car was running by glancing at the speedometer, and the conversation turned to the plans for a vaudeville tour which was to begin the following week with an engagement in New York City.

Next day Johnson put his money in the First National Bank, and three days later he and Etta boarded the Twentieth Century Limited. At this time, Jack's career appeared to be moving as smoothly as that famous train on its specially inspected roadbed. After the violent night that followed the match in Reno, it seemed that the air had cleared and that Johnson had a chance to become a respected celebrity. Some people thought it just might be that Johnson had developed a sense of responsibility, and that being the indisputable heavyweight champion of the world would somehow improve his character, and tone him down, and make him more generally acceptable. Two things argued for this view: one, that his homecoming had shown how well he provided for his family, and the other, the national disappointment in Jeffries, which by a

paradox of human nature now made a lot of people begin
to tell themselves that Jack was not as bad as they had
thought.

In the matter of Jeffries, it is hard to find an instance
of a man in any field falling so far and so rapidly in public
esteem. To begin with, let us see what those who were
close to him had to say. Tex Rickard remarked, "Jeff was
in great shape so far as running miles on the road was
concerned, but he did not spar enough for us to guess
how he would show up on the firing line." Corbett
growled, "Jeffries would have done better in a marathon
race than a prize fight." Muldoon said, "The fight looked
like a professor of boxing giving a lesson to a stupid
pupil. Jeffries' trouble was lack of coordination between
mind and muscle. The muscles were there and preparing
to perform their functions, but the connections were bad.
Long brooding had deranged his entire nervous system
and although his mind and muscles were in perfect order
they did not work in harmony." Sullivan said, "Jeff wasn't
in it. This will probably be the last big fight."

So spoke the oracles of the profession. Their interpreters,
the newspaper experts, had in most cases been flatly
wrong, and now displayed an understandable distaste for
the loser. When describing Johnson they now spoke of
black panthers and streaks of lightning, but in referring
to Jeffries, they searched the dictionary for words denot-
ing crass ineptitude. Only a few had no need to change
tune: Tad Dorgan had predicted Johnson's victory, as
had the cartoonist Rube Goldberg. And John I. Day contributed his usual good sense to the summing up: "It
was the statements issued by the said experts, with one or

two notable exceptions, that kept the fond hopes of the white man's admirers at the boiling point, and made the bitter dose of defeat all the tougher to swallow. There have been plenty of cases where the favorite went down to defeat, but none where the favorite's boosters were made to look so sublimely ridiculous. Jeffries was just an inert bulk of brawn and muscle, that lumbered stupidly, destitute of the slightest spark of fighting fire. His big, brainless head simply rocked to and fro under the impact of Johnson's gloves. Talk about the intellectual superiority of the white to the black man! It exists in the majority of cases to be sure; but here was one instance where the exception shone forth brilliantly. There was as much difference between Jeffries' ability to think and perform and Johnson's, as there is between the turgid perception and movements of an East Indian government army bullock and the lightning attack of a Bengal tiger."

Much of the disappointment and resentment over Jeffries' defeat took the form of denouncing the entire affair as an outbreak of brutality. In this the professional journalists were outdone by the writers of letters to the editor who crowded the correspondence columns with expressions of horror and alarm. Though "no mollycoddle," a writer to *The New York Times* called the fight and its result "a calamity to this country worse than the San Francisco earthquake." A reader of the *New York Herald* inquired, "Has not prizefighting become a *reductio ad absurdum* when the best fighter comes from the lowest and least developed race among us?" And from Brooklyn, "Righteous Indignation" made the *Times* letter column by pointing out that blood had been shed throughout the nation merely because "two brutes, one white, the other black . . . pummeled each other publicly to the delectation of other brutes." And the *New York Tribune* published a letter that ended, "Some people may not like to see a black American win. But, beware of Japan! The worst is yet to come!"

In the rear of the reporters and reader-correspondents came the editorial writers, who on first reception of the news from Reno unanimously struck the note of deprecating horror. The *Times* set the tone: "The fight proved nothing more than that one human brute is more alert and stronger than another. The black human 'outbruted' the white."

One of the most interesting aspects of the newspaper comments on the Reno fight was its exploding of the myth that there was more intelligence and common sense in the brains of Englishmen than could be found in the United States. The *London Daily Telegraph* led off: "The days of the ring are over. Whatever glories it once possessed have vanished. The Reno encounter was deplorable not only because it was disgusting, but because it aggravates the color problem." The *London Daily News* chimed in with regrets that "the most sacred day of the American civil calendar should be celebrated before the whole world by the most nakedly commercial prize fight in the history of pugilism. The only hopeful light about the affair is the growth of the American resolve that this shall be the last." From *The London Times* came a solemn honking that "if the old-fashioned, straight-forward fighting had prevailed at Reno, Jeffries would never have been knocked down." All told, the British papers had given more space to the Johnson-Jeffries fight than to the relief of Mafeking in the Boer War.

After a few days passed, the editors in New York and the other large cities of the United States found their high blood pressure over Johnson's victory receding, and in most cases decided that another look at the entire situation was in order. Having devoted thousands of columns and millions of words to the fight, they could not now simply dismiss it, and while it was under discussion, they wanted to set the racial aspect of it straight. Typical of these second-look editorials was one which appeared on July 6 in *The New York Times*; it is interesting today as evidence that the eyes of white Americans were not totally blinded by color prejudice in the year 1910. This historically important statement in the *Times* began with the observation that "intelligent and self-supporting Negroes" might think Johnson's victory a misfortune, since it might encourage young Negroes to go into prizefighting rather than respectable trades. Also, it "stirred the animosity of a lower class of whites." But, the newspaper continued, "there is another view of the matter which will appeal to the independent judgment of all fairminded white men in all sections of the country. It is that the Negro, in the low arena in which he was challenged by the white man, had held his part with entire credit. Johnson showed not only that he had greater available strength and endurance than Jeffries, but that he brought to his task greater intelligence and skill, a sounder judgment, equal courage, and a perfectly fair, manly, and honorable standard of behavior. . . . It is to be noted that in the whole field of activity in this country there has been a strong tendency to confine the

Negroes to occupations of lower grades, analogous to that of the ring, in which mere strength is employed, and to shut them out of those in which the higher qualities are required and attained. That a representative of the race should win a substantial triumph in the lowest of these will instinctively be recognized as meaning to members of the race a somewhat different and higher title to respect. The sentiment that has developed the rules of the ring—on the whole a sentiment of fair play, a desire to make certain that the really better man should win—will tend toward this respect in the very classes where race animosity has been most bitter and unreasoning." Perhaps feeling that he was beginning to break up on the reefs of generality, the *Times* editorialist now steered in a discussion of Booker T. Washington's doctrine that every Negro should devote most of his energy to making the best progress of which he was capable in the most lucrative trade he could find open to him. According to the *Times,* Washington had taught that all the Negro needed was a chance at fair economic competition. "It is quite within the range of reasonable expectation," the paper went on, "that the indirect influence of the black man's victory in the prize ring, where the conditions of strife were rudely but practically framed on the basis of equality and fairness, may be to stimulate respect for quality and fairness in more respectable competitions. In that case an occurrence ignoble enough may prove to have a redeeming effect."

A fair, manly, and honorable standard of behavior! By no means undeserved insofar as they applied to Johnson's conduct in the ring against Jeffries, these generous words were echoed by the *Times*' Reno correspondent. John L. Sullivan completed his fight assignment by saying he saw little that was petty or mean in Johnson's character. He continued, "In spite of my well-known antipathy to his race, I must say that he played fairly and at all times fought fairly. He gave in whenever there was a contention, and he demanded his rights only up to their limit, but never beyond it."

This represented the high point of Jack Johnson's public esteem, white division. Among black people, his word on any subject would have been interpreted as binding law. And while the train loped across Indiana, scores of Negroes were going through the black belts of New York and Brooklyn, distributing thousands of handbills that read: "TO EVERY COLORED MAN, WOMAN OR CHILD IN GREATER NEW YORK, BE AT GRAND CENTRAL STATION AT 9:30 O'CLOCK MONDAY MORNING, AND LET US ALL SHAKE THE HAND OF THE STALWART ATHLETE, THE GREATEST OF THE TWENTIETH CENTURY. COME ANY WAY YOU CAN. COME IN VEHICLES OR ON FOOT. ALL BE THERE."

As at Chicago, Johnson was late getting into New York City, this time because of a wreck on the line, which caused a five hour delay. What makes this detail worth recording is the fact that 10,000 Negroes were still at Grand Central Station when the Twentieth Century Limited finally got in. Except for a few collapses because of heat and pushing in the crowd, nobody was hurt. Johnson smiled, waved, bowed, stepped into a high-powered car, and rolled away to a hotel kept by a friend in Harlem.

Etta went along; since meeting Johnson, she had spent her
life in the world of Negroes, and would continue to do so
for the time remaining to her. During this period, Johnson
made his widely quoted explanation of why he preferred
white women. Forgetting his beloved mother, Jack said
he "couldn't get along" with Negro women, because he
"couldn't trust them."

Something else Johnson did not trust was the possibility
of making a fortune from the rental of the motion pictures
taken at Reno. As we have seen, both Jeffries and Johnson
sold their shares in future cinema royalties for cash in
hand; and so they could now look with perfect equanimity
on the widely organized reformers' campaign against the
showing of the films. The strength of this anti-fight-film
movement was at the Protestant churches, as was shown
by the Christian Endeavor Young People's Society, a
nationwide apparatus for harnessing the energies of teen-
agers for good works. Johnson was still in Chicago when
this group announced that it was opposing "the reproduc-
tion of this barbarous fight in thousands of moving picture
shows [theaters], where the minds of the boys and girls,
the future citizens of America, will be tainted, corrupted,
and brutalized by such scenes."

For once Rickard had guessed wrong. He thought the
holding of the fight had represented a victory, with the
forces of reform driven from the field. It was a victory,
but of a skirmish only; and his fight films, so to speak, now
represented a hostage in the hands of powerful and respectable forces, like the adult leaders of the Christian Endeavorers, who pointed out that "Millions of upright and
decent young people stood in need of protection against

the agents of the pugilistic world, of which both principals and promoters were composed of the coarsest elements in the country." Eloquent with indignation, speakers and writers took up the argument, in the tone of the New York minister who said, "Every state in the union, with the exception of little Nevada, refused to allow the fight. Now let these states show a similar sense of morality by not allowing the motion pictures of this deplorable and savage exhibition to be displayed." Such influential voices kept repeating the idea until it was a slogan: *The fight pictures will be worse than the fight!* This generated the degree of heat that gives unbearable discomfort to politicians, and their agitated braying soon filled the air. "This is a nightmare!" cried the mayor of Philadelphia, as he tried to avoid the spokesmen of civic groups encamped before his doors to compel him to order the fight films out of town. In San Francisco, Mayor McCarthy was one of the few municipal officers to permit the full and immediate showing of the pictures. In Chicago, traditionally an open town, City Hall tried to straddle with talk about an "expurgated version" of Rickard's movies. This showed the might of the Cook County reform movement and of Arthur Burrage Farwell's Law and Order League, which had already lined up beside the Christian Endeavorers. The pain of the politicians was intense, for they could smell the money, yet in most cases feared to accept the graft that would soak up to them, just as it does today, from the licensing officials and collection men. Picture a glutton confronted by a large helping of Tripes à la mode de Caen, but with his hands tied, and one can feel some of the anguish of the mayors of Boston, Atlanta,

Baltimore, St. Louis, and Cincinnati, to name but a few, who ran into the same difficulties over the licensing of Rickard's films as Gillett of California had met in connection with Rickard's fight. In New York, Mayor Gaynor followed the same course as his Chicago colleague by muttering about the possibility of allowing an edited version to be shown. Gaynor failed to specify what would be cut: it would be easy to dispense with shots of Sam Berger, Sig Hart, and Uncle Billy Jordan; but one could hardly charge admission for moving pictures of the fight without showing the collapse of Jeffries from repeated blows to the face and body. In any event, the municipal authorities were soon relieved of responsibility by the passage in Congress of a law making it a Federal offense to transport moving pictures of prize fights across a state line.

This legislation against the movement of fight pictures resembled the Mann Act, a law that forbade interstate transportation of women for immoral purposes. The reformers of America believed that vice lords in the big cities were holding thousands of women to involuntary prostitution, and Representative James Robert Mann* of Illinois wrote the Act that bears his name to put these "white slavers" out of business and into jail. Though it was poorly

---

* Born on a farm in central Illinois, Mann served in Congress for 25 years. He took himself with immense seriousness, and like Gillett of California once thought he might be headed for the White House. At the time his Act became law, Mann's home in Oak Park was near that of the architect Frank Lloyd Wright. Some years later, in a startling misuse of Federal power, Wright was made a victim of his old neighbor's legislation, spending two days in a Minneapolis jail before the government men came to their senses.

conceived and awkwardly drawn, Mann's "White Slave Traffic Act," as it was titled, got through Congress in June of 1910. Though busy preparing for Jeffries at the time, Jack Johnson might have done well to follow the debate. He would have agreed with Representatives W. C. Adamson, William Richardson, and C. R. Bartlett, who protested that "Congress cannot in the exercise of police power punish citizens of the states for violating a Federal statute made under the pretense of regulating morals and suppressing evils which in the strictest and most literal sense, along with health, peace, and order, is an affair that belongs to the states; and the Federal Government never has and never can, under our existing Federal system, lawfully claim or exercise such power, except in the District of Columbia and the Territories."

Though in the minority, these men gave good reasons why the Mann Act might be called a dubious piece of legislation. Three days after its passage, a highly respectable voice was heard in New York City, saying that there was not even any need for such a law. The spokesman was John D. Rockefeller, Jr., who had served as foreman on a special grand jury investigating commercialized vice. Too modest to enter politics, Rockefeller had a high-derbied integrity that added weight to the jury's report. The document said that after six months of investigation, the jurors found that there was no organized trade in women in New York City. The Rockefeller panel took this as almost certain exoneration of the other large American cities, so far as involuntary prostitution was concerned, since those who believed in a nationwide white slave industry also maintained that New

York City was the staging area for the rest of the country. Nevertheless, the Mann Act became operative.

But so far as Johnson was concerned, all these things might as well have happened on the moon. He continued to prance around New York City, feeling exceptionally fine and not caring whether Rickard exhibited the films or cut them up into celluloid collars and mandolin picks. He did not consider himself one of those symbolic people through whom an issue is drawn and presented to the world. All the same, he was becoming such a person, and the questions that impinged on him were only partly racial. As in the case of Dred Scott, Johnson was to play a role in a discussion that had moral, economic, political, and constitutional aspects. The reform movement, abolition's direct descendant, had more to it than resolutions passed by the young members of Christian Endeavor. It had the blind fervor that can lead to war; for just as the Massachusetts Emigrant Aid Society had put aggressive abolitionist farmers into Kansas fifty years before, the Law and Order Leagues and the Anti-Saloon League of Wayne B. Wheeler now sent out bands of private detectives to hunt for immoral persons, and illegal sellers of whiskey. Deputized with police powers, these detectives were the sort who had sufficient hardihood to break strikes when not engaged in raiding speakeasies, and they were rough and dangerous men.

Four days after the fight at Reno, Wheeler's private detectives started a civil war in Newark, a central Ohio city of something over twenty-five thousand inhabitants. So far as the sale of liquor was concerned, most people in Newark and Licking County were satisfied, as the entire region was dry by local option, yet there was plenty of beer and whiskey to be had at thinly disguised places known as soft drink saloons.

One of the most popular of these resorts was a tavern on the edge of town called The Last Chance. Its proprietor, William Howard, had hundreds of friends in Newark and the adjacent farming country. Standing behind his bar on the night of July 8, Howard looked up to see a group of strangers entering the taproom. Announcing themselves as deputized raiders from the Anti-Saloon League, they told Howard he was under arrest for violating the local option prohibition law. Howard said, "Let's see your warrants." The detectives produced search-and-seizure papers signed by the mayor of Granville, a nearby Baptist college town. "Not enough law," said Howard. There was a scuffle, and a raider named Carl Etherington shot Howard dead. The word spread through Newark and hundreds of men armed with rifles and shotguns hurried to the center of town. The deputies took refuge in the city jail and sent word to the governor asking for a declaration of martial law. When this news got back to Newark, a citizens' committee entered the jail, took out Etherington, and hanged him to a telegraph pole. Next morning Edward Hale, chief of the Anti-Saloon League's combat arm, announced that Wheeler had ordered him to send fifty heavily armed men to Newark to arrest the city officials. This finally brought action to the state capital, and the governor dispatched National Guard troops to Newark, at the same time begging Wheeler to go easy for a while. There is no evidence that Johnson read the Newark dispatches, but they added to Sig Hart's feeling of anxiety and impending doom. Hart said, "Those reformers don't fool around."

One reason Johnson paid no attention to events in Ohio was that he was busy arranging a tour of the music halls in Europe. This was easy money, and he liked the trouper's life. Accordingly he and Etta rehearsed a version of their act containing new material on Jeffries; the little men with the cigars were pleased, and Jack's party left to fill bookings in London, Marseilles, Lyons, Paris, Brussels, Berlin, Budapest, Bucharest, and St. Petersburg. Managing the troupe was Jack's nephew Gus Rhodes, an agreeable young man with considerable diplomatic ability. This he needed when Johnson's euphoria became so great that he gave offense to those around him by sheer noise and disorder. His first appearances on this trip were in England, where he was an object of curiosity; his optimism was so great that he refused to be aware of an unfriendly undercurrent in some of the crowds that came to see him perform. "I was a bigger attraction than the king," said the champion, referring to his arrival in England during the coronation of George V. It was true that Johnson got plenty of attention, and some of it offstage, as when the landlady of Loughborough House, an apartment hotel on Northumberland Street in Paddington, came to court with a tale of smashed crockery and broken furniture. It would seem that Johnson was the pilot model for the type of rowdy and destructive celebrity from the sporting and theatrical world that is taken for granted today. It may be noted, therefore, that Jack Johnson occupies a significant place in the history of disorderly conduct, marking the spot where show business celebrities first took up

the tradition of public nuisance handed down from the
bucks and rakes of Victorian and Regency days.

Though Johnson fell far short of many eminent movie
actors in vanity, petulance, and meanness, he could cause
excitement at any pleasure resort merely by putting in an
appearance. His entrance into a London or Paris supper
club was impressive, for he always had with him a party
of from six to twenty people, and the group would be the
center of a scurry of waiters and wine stewards. He was
frequently photographed at table, surrounded by smiling
dark and light faces, and usually grinning at the camera
over a clump of bottles. Sometimes the guests at Johnson's
table were as interesting as the host; one drinking companion was the Rev. Mr. Harold Davidson, the Rector of
Stiffkey (pronounced Stewkey), who was later disfrocked
for gross impropriety, after which he became a sideshow
attraction at the British seaside resorts.

Johnson was conscious of the difference between these
surroundings and those of his hoboing youth, and the
contrast set him thinking of a profitable way to dramatize
his extraordinary advance in the world. Meditating in the
fine restaurants and cabarets of London, Paris, and Berlin
on the distance he had traveled since his Galveston childhood, Johnson decided he could be happy as the managing director of a luxurious saloon. He was by no means
the first pugilist to think of opening a tavern. The custom
was established so well that it was mentioned in Bernard
Shaw's novel about a prizefighter, *Cashel Byron's Profession,* by a character who remarked of the boxer as a type
that "If he has saved money he opens a sporting public-
house, where he sells spirits of the worst description to

his old rivals and their associates, and eventually drinks himself to death or bankruptcy." Johnson planned to do better than that, in every way. What he had in mind was to add to the nearly eight thousand saloons of Chicago a handsomely furnished, racially integrated cabaret-restaurant, where the management would not try to dictate the patrons' conduct. Jack's idea was that with such a place available and open all night, there might be, as he put it, "some lively times."

Johnson had no cash for this investment; his money went out as fast as it came in, for he could easily spend a thousand dollars a day on first class travel and luxury hotels. Financial backing came from a brewery, enabling him to open his Chicago place on a balmy October evening in 1911. He had named the establishment Café de Champion, in Cook County French, and he had chosen a good spot for it at 42 West 31st Street, immediately to the south of the Levee district, an area that was notorious for its brothels, saloons, and low dance halls. A man would hardly invite a woman to accompany him into the Levee itself; but the location of Jack's place was acceptable. Johnson had skillfully obtained publicity well in advance, so it was no surprise that a block-long line of customers stood waiting to get in when Johnson threw open the doors of the Café de Champion.

The patrons found themselves in a sumptuous establishment with five spacious rooms, a tremendous bar, solid silver cuspidors, and a great number of paintings and other art works on display. "Having traveled extensively," Johnson said of this episode in his memoirs, "I had gained a comprehensive idea of decorative effects. I also had collected many fine works of art, curios, and novelties, an array of artistic creations which put to shame many similar establishments in both Europe and America." Visitors viewed portraits of Johnson, his wife, and his parents by "one of the foremost artists in America." The proprietor pointed out "a few real Rembrandts" which he had picked up in Europe, and a series of Biblical scenes, together with a life-size representation of the Empress Cleopatra at the height of her reign. As they inspected the luxurious place, a spirit of festival descended on the customers. It may have been inspired by the gold of Johnson's smile, or the heartiness of his chuckle; at any rate, to use Johnson's words, "The celebration was one which will long be remembered."

Some of the memories were to come from the effects of the Rajah's peg, which Jack recommended to all who could get near him in the crowd. Other customers swigged wine, gin, vodka, whiskey and ale in such quantities that the wholesalers had to bring in an entire new stock the following day. While this ocean of drink was being consumed, entertainers sang the current hits, including "Some of These Days," "That's Why They Call Me Shine," and "The Whiffenpoof Song." The noise itself seemed to hold people up; and the sun had risen before the last bartender collapsed with a cramp in his bottle hand, and the last customer tottered off home. Lively times, indeed; and business at the Café de Champion was to continue at this astonishing pace night and day.

On the second floor of the café, at the end of the hall from a pair of private dining rooms, was the apartment occupied by Jack and Etta, who had been married, as we know, the previous February. With these living arrangements, Jack could go for weeks without seeing daylight or going outside. His duty as proprietor was merely to show himself around the place, as the work of management was delegated to a major-domo named Toots Marshall. Johnson had no reason to go into training, for no opponent worth looking at appeared among the white hopes, as the newspapers called non-Negro heavyweight challengers. Johnson was shrewd. He knew there was no chance of drawing a large crowd to see him defeat a mediocre opponent. They would pay in large numbers only to see Jack lose. The hopes were sturdy enough, but they lacked skill. Most of the ranch hands, freight hustlers, shacks, and lumbermen who turned to the ring for the specific purpose of challenging Johnson had little idea what they were getting into. They were the type of Carl Morris, a 240-pound railroad engineer who left the cab the morning after the Burns fight to announce that he was now a professional boxer and would "restore the title to the white race." He had no talent and got nowhere. More recently Johnson had observed that another enormous man, named Jess Willard, was trying to learn the game; he came from Pottawatomie County, Kansas. Johnson surmised that he was just a rube who would soon disappear. The golden belt that symbolized the championship remained on display in Johnson's bar.

In the spring of 1912, a man with a businesslike air called on Johnson and said he wanted to talk about money. Johnson paid close attention, as he always did when this subject was under discussion. The visitor was Jack Curley, an experienced promoter who had risen, like

Jack himself, from humble circumstances. Born in San Francisco in 1876, Curley was to go so high in the world that he would entertain Edward VIII as Prince of Wales at his Long Island mansion. His Alsatian parents had named him Jacques Armand, and he took the name of Jack Curley when he entered the prize ring as a middle-weight around the turn of the century. After a brief boxing career he turned promoter, and among other successful projects once arranged a lecture tour for William Jennings Bryan. When he met Johnson, Curley was known around Chicago for his share in putting on the Gotsch-Hackenschmidt wrestling match at Comiskey Park in 1911, which was ruled a fraud, and caused professional wrestling to be barred from Illinois for many years.

Jack Curley had no intention of suggesting a dubious deal to Johnson. It simply seemed to him unjust that a world champion should go almost two years without a fight. Johnson told Curley that he felt the same way: while abroad he had almost brought off a match with Bombardier Billy Wells, an English heavyweight who had a large following. Wells had won the approval of Sir William Eden, who pronounced his evening clothes faultless. It was Sir William, as we recall, who objected to the dinner jacket worn by the president of the National Sporting Club. Indeed, Wells lacked only one thing—a hard punch with his left or right fist. For this reason the London County Council refused to license the fight, or so Jack Johnson saw it. He summed it up to Curley, "Nobody wants to see me win."

Curley understood very well; and he had a suggestion: why not fight Fireman Jim Flynn? He was referring to the rugged heavyweight whose true name was Andrew Chiariglione. Johnson had fought Flynn in 1907; he recalled that the Fireman had stood up well for eleven rounds, then left himself open to a knockout blow. Could he now be presented to the public as a plausible contender? Curley thought so; and Johnson was persuaded.

The fight took place in Las Vegas exactly two years after the Reno match. But the publicity build-up of Fireman Jim Flynn had failed, and there were less than five thousand spectators. Moreover, Flynn had deteriorated since the last time he faced Johnson. At Las Vegas, he lasted only till the ninth round, when he was floundering about, confused and helpless, and the police stopped the fight for fear of injury; it was a repetition of the match with Tommy Burns. Disappointed with the small audience, Johnson was pleased by the thought that he would some day get into a profitable deal with the help of Jack Curley. He had respect for this man and paid attention when Curley told him the same thing Sig Hart had said so many times: watch out for those reformers around Cook County.

Jack heard his knowing advisers but he did not act. Meanwhile, an interesting development was unfolding as the reformers in northern Illinois continued to assemble what sociologists would nowadays refer to as a power structure. The Law and Order Leagues of Cook County had combined into one association with Arthur Burrage Farwell at its head. He now drew up a report showing that no less than thirty-eight other religious and civic organizations—not mere letterhead outfits, but earnest groups of working agitators—were in the field under

League supervision, to increase and continue the political and social assault on vice, crime, and civic irregularity. The report noted many things that showed the League's power: for example, it had brought about the cancellation of the First Ward Ball, a time-honored annual event through which politicians raised money by selling tickets to saloonkeepers, prostitutes, and men who liked to dress as women. What probably pleased Farwell most, however, was being able to announce the arrival in town of an "extra force of Federal agents" who would assist in tracking down violators of the Mann Act. On their first day they arrested a noted pander, Madam Nettie Jackson, with five girls on a Chicago, Milwaukee & St. Paul passenger train bound for Houghton, Michigan.

Farwell had supporters who were willing to attack the strongholds of vice without the aid of Federal men. Typical of these activists was a young suburbanite named Virginia Brooks, whom the *Chicago American* was to name the Joan of Arc of West Hammond, Indiana. Miss Brooks came to public attention by announcing that she had marked down eight vice lords of West Hammond to be tarred and feathered, and ridden out of town on a rail. She said this would be done by a committee of fifty women carrying shotguns and revolvers. The sheriff persuaded Virginia Brooks not to lead out armed forces in West Hammond, and she came to Chicago, to become a power among the militant reformers.

In the state capital, legislators and officials were feeling the pressure toward taking legal measures for moral reform, and they went into action, passing a bill drawn up by Lieutenant-Governor Barratt O'Hara, a former newspaperman, establishing a State Commission to investigate vice and crime, and bring malefactors to justice. It was obvious that the Commission's major field of activity would be Cook County, but this did not keep Arthur Farwell and other crusaders from establishing their own Committee of Fifteen to gather evidence against "lawless saloonkeepers and the lords of commercialized vice." This Committee had power behind it: besides Farwell and his followers, it numbered among its sponsors the heads of the Civic Reform Association and the Chicago Vigilance Association, the editors of the daily papers, and the eloquent and zealous Rev. Dr. M. E. Williams of Grace Methodist Episcopal Church. Imposing as they were, these were not all the forces marshaled against the sporting people of Chicago: even more ominous was the special grand jury convened by United States Attorney John E. W. Wyman to hand down indictments against the many culprits he expected to have within his grasp.

Two months after the Flynn fight, Etta decided to take a brief vacation from Johnson and the Café de Champion. She planned to go for her holiday to Las Vegas, accompanied by a Chicago sports writer's wife, and leaving on the evening of September 11. An hour before the time of departure, Etta said she had become so ill from a headache that she would have to take a later train, and Jack offered to go to the station to explain Etta's absence to her friend. When he got back at about ten-thirty, he saw a crowd in front of the café, and a police car. He hurried upstairs, burst into the apartment, and found his wife's maids Helen Simmons and Mabel Bolden with uniformed police and detectives. They had terrible news: shortly after Johnson left for the station, Etta had dressed herself in a night-gown and dismissed the women. As she closed her bed-room door, she said, "Pray for me." The maids then heard a shot, ran into the bedroom, and found Etta unconscious; she had shot herself in the head. Helen Simmons dashed downstairs and told Toots Marshall, who telephoned for police and an ambulance. Etta was now dying at Provident Hospital. Jack's mother and sisters were already there.

Too dazed to order the café closed or the music stopped, Johnson hurried back through the crowd to his car, where Gus Rhodes sat at the wheel. As he crossed the sidewalk he wept and held a large handkerchief to his eyes. A Negro on the edge of the crowd called out: "A bawling cow soon forgets her calf."

Etta did not regain consciousness, and died early the following morning. Two days later her body was taken from Jack's Wabash Avenue house to St. Mark's African Methodist Episcopal Church at Fiftieth Street, seventeen blocks south. Etta's mother and sister were the only white persons at the services, where they heard the choir sing Etta's favorite hymn, "Take the Name of Jesus with You." Pastor John W. Robinson preached a funeral sermon, at one point asking, "Is there anyone in this church who can be so cruel as to deny the star of hope to the weary one? Is there any who cannot let the great mantle of charity cover the call of a disquieted heart?"

They buried Etta Terry Duryea Johnson in Graceland Cemetery. But the question of whether Johnson's rowdy and untidy manner of living had driven her to suicide was not so easily laid to rest. Jack Curley pointed out that

Etta had been grieved by the recent death of her father. He also said that although Etta was "a happy woman" she had a tendency "to become overconcerned about things." Her doctor said she had suffered nervous prostration. Johnson said Etta must have been insane when she shot herself. He added that so far as he knew she was never despondent, and he could say it for a certainty, as he knew what depression was: once not long after the Jeffries fight he had suffered such an attack of melancholy that he started to choke himself to death in a hotel room. Etta had persuaded him not to hurt himself, and bathed his face with cold wine.

Johnson wept; but within a month he was in trouble with one of the café entertainers, a handsome mulatto singer named Adah Banks. Miss Banks shot Johnson in the foot during an argument over his attentions to a white girl named Lucille Cameron. The injury was negligible, but the situation that brought it about contained the seeds of disaster. Lucille Cameron, a bright, good-looking girl, had come to Chicago from Minneapolis at the age of nineteen to see life and get on in the world. She visited the Café de Champion, introduced herself to Johnson, and got a job as secretary and bookkeeper in the restaurant. Lucille's mother, Mrs. Cameron-Falconet, followed within a few weeks and announced that she intended to charge Johnson with abducting Lucille. Her chief council was a Chicago lawyer named Charley Erbstein, who engaged in a shouting match with Johnson at the main bar of the café. The encounter ended with Jack threatening bodily harm, and Erbstein threatening the rigors of the law. In giving his account of the dispute to the newspapers, Erb-

stein said, "I think we can get Johnson on the Mann Act."
All he got at the time was an indictment on the abduction
charge. Safe from the wrath of that vanished court, one
may now venture to express amazement that this accusation was ever entertained at law, as Johnson had never
heard of Lucille Cameron before she walked into his
saloon. Girls like Lucille Cameron came to big cities every
day: the fact had been noted as long before as 1900 by
Theodore Dreiser in his novel, *Sister Carrie*. It was true
that the publisher decided the novel exceeded the bounds
of respectability, and suppressed it; nevertheless, Lucille
Cameron might have stepped from its pages. But even if
compelled to admit that coming to Chicago had been
Lucille's idea alone, Mrs. Cameron-Falconet would never
concede that the girl was staying in the city voluntarily.
"Jack Johnson has hypnotic powers," said the mother,
"and he has exercised them on my little girl."

In point of fact, there was no more evidence of intimacy
between Lucille and Johnson than there was of hypnotic
control on his part; the girl behaved with discretion, and
was living at Jack Curley's house. For all of that, the
Federal authorities arrested Lucille and confined her to
a hotel room with armed guards outside the door. This
was to "keep her out of Johnson's clutches." And in order
to "forestall legal technicalities," that is, any discussion of
Lucille's constitutional rights, the authorities set her bail
at $25,000. Johnson drew this sum at the First National
Bank; the news spread in the Loop, and a crowd hung
around the building for three hours after Johnson had
gone, and long after the court had ruled that he was not
a proper person to put up bail for Lucille Cameron. There

was a restless feeling in Chicago that hazy October afternoon; a mile or so north of the bank, a crowd hanged a
dummy labeled "Johnson." Some of the men held up a
sign that read, "IF ONLY WE HAD A REAL NEGRO."

Jack was on the public mind. And there was a general
making up of that mind into hardened opinion that could
be expressed in a few words. "He's gone too far," a man
would say, and anyone hearing the remark would know
who was referred to. Etta's suicide, the continuing uproar
at the Café de Champion, frequent arrests and fines for
speeding—and now this matter of Lucille Cameron; it was
too much. And the rising pressure for reform made Johnson and his conduct even more noticeable than it might
have been when there was less general excitement about
morality, vice, and crime. Said the *Inter-Ocean*: "Popular
indignation over the numerous outrages on public morals
perpetrated by 'Jack' Johnson, the Negro prize fighter, has
reached such a stage that it is dangerous for him to walk
in the public streets."

At the time of Lucille's arrest, the public streets were the
scene of a demonstration which should have convinced
Johnson that the moment to leave Chicago had arrived.
This was the great anti-vice parade put on by the combined civic welfare associations of Cook County; Virginia
Brooks was grand marshal, working under Arthur Farwell's direction and with the help of more separate groups
than can be counted, for more than forty thousand people
marched the South Side entertainment districts in an
unmistakable threat of action that was emphasized by
the troop of mounted police which rode at the head of the
line. This procession had an immediate effect on many

who saw it: a number of the pimps, whores, and gamblers who watched it pass went to their lodgings, packed their suitcases, and quietly left town. And well they might: for on the heels of the police had marched a delegation of 200 ministers in silk hats and Prince Albert coats, led by the Committee of Fifteen's Dr. Williams and singing "Onward Christian Soldiers." Next had appeared large marching bodies of Boy Scouts, Girl Scouts, members of the Epworth League, the Women's Christian Temperance Union, and the Catholic Temperance Society, together with students from the Baptist Missionary Training School and numerous Moody Bible Institutes.

Interspersed with the detachments of marchers were floats carrying banners and living pictures aimed at the saloon trade and allied industries. One warned against smoking with an enormous sign which stated that the Chicago Cubs "must cut out cigarettes." The Norwegian churches contributed a scene with twelve armored knights guarding an athlete in pink tights who carried a sign reading: "The Great God Thor with his hammer. The Norwegians will help smite the saloons."

The military formation of this parade promised militant zeal in ridding Chicago of wrongdoers; but the marchers were only the uniformed ranks of reform's army, identifiable by clerical dress or equally unmistakable signs. The war on wickedness also made use of plainclothes troops— the specially deputized detectives—who played the roles of spies and raiding partisans. These guerilla troops were effective, but sometimes attacked innocent people. One can hardly believe anything was accomplished, for example, when agents of the Illinois Vice Commission

arrested students from Northwestern and the Universities
of Chicago and Indiana at Madam Victoria Shaw's establishment. Indeed, nothing *was* accomplished—except
the ruin of the young men's careers. An interesting by-
product, to be sure, but not likely to contribute to the
freeing of the white slaves. And the reformers made no
converts of the married couple, occupying a room in a
South Side hotel, on whom they intruded in the middle
of the night. When the husband asked if they had a
warrant, the vice detectives said, "We don't need a warrant." The raiders had been drinking, and their conduct
was so rough and their language so abusive that the young
wife collapsed in hysterics and a doctor had to be called.

All this would seem illegal enough to rouse the least
sensitive defender of civil liberties, but when it came to
illegality, most newspapers and their readers seemed to
feel that the "vice lords" were the ones who were violating
the law, though, in the absence of statutes forbidding
prostitution, it was hard to see what laws they had broken,
provided their behavior was orderly. As to Johnson, he
of course was the worst of all; and J. W. Bragdon, a substantial Minneapolis businessman, spoke for a large section
of established opinion when he wrote to the editors of his
home city and Chicago: "A blur has been brought upon
the fair name of Minneapolis. As president and secretary
of the Minneapolis Commercial Club, we appeal to your
sense of justice to do what is in your power to obliterate
the attempts of this notorious, obnoxious individual to get
into the public press. His defiance of the law, disregard of
clean morals and his other numerous crimes should not
be tolerated or put forth in public print. It is time suppres-

sion should be made. There should be a general protest of this character."

While Jack Johnson might have been willing to forego his accustomed publicity at this time, there was no question how the editors felt. They would have been as willing to give up mentioning Johnson as they would to surrender the keys to the desk drawers containing their breakfast whiskey. In this matter the seasoned executive journalist's attitude was expressed by Ed Conkle, head of the Chicago United Press office and the son of a Methodist minister, when he said to his men, "Keep that vice stuff coming. People like to read about what they like to do." And whether or not that aspect of the matter had drawn the attention of Booker T. Washington, this acknowledged spokesman for American Negroes joined the chorus in criticism of Jack Johnson. Speaking before the Detroit Young Men's Christian Association, Washington said, "Jack Johnson has harmed rather than helped the race. I wish to say emphatically that his actions do not meet my approval, and I'm sure they do not meet with the approval of the colored race."

In the general uproar about morals, white slaves, gamblers, and Jack Johnson, some of the scarifying public criticism fell on persons far more respectable than Johnson; and their surprise at being singled out was equaled only by their indignation. Such was the experience of the philanthropist Julius Rosenwald, founder of the Sears, Roebuck mail order house. It was during this period that Rosenwald came before the Illinois Vice Commission to protest against the semi-official theory that prostitution resulted from the small wages paid by large firms. When

he came into the hearing-room, Rosenwald's commonplace
appearance belied his wealth and power; with his rimless
glasses and toothbrush mustache, he looked like the hum-
bler sort of bookkeeper. But like a good bookkeeper, he
had the figures in his head, and his testimony produced
a powerful effect on his hearers.

It was not true, said the magnate, that Sears, Roebuck
paid its women employees less than eight dollars a week.
The facts were that the company had a number of be-
ginners or apprentices at from five to eight dollars a week;
these were girls of seventeen and under. There were 119
fifteen- and sixteen-year-old apprentices earning five dollars a week. But more than one thousand women employees had savings accounts; and there were 3,267
women earning an average of $10.20 per week. Among
these women, the minimum wage was eight dollars a week.
To this witness's way of thinking, it was therefore the
most deplorable sort of headline hunting for the Commission to talk of Rosenwald paying less than eight dollars
a week. However, he admitted having a total of 4,700
women employees, and the onlookers could not help making a mental calculation which showed Rosenwald was
conceding that he paid some fourteen hundred women
less than eight dollars a week. One thing was certain:
Rosenwald was not offering the vice kings any competition
for the services of young women and girls. Perhaps the
only conclusion that can now be drawn is that philanthro-
pists should not be subjected to criticism, but left alone
to do good in their own way.

Johnson's philanthropy was the practical and immediate
kind, as he showed when he helped get Clara Kerr back

on her feet. Usually it took the form of large tips and paying the bills at drinking parties. This form of generosity was no recommendation for the mercies of the Federal grand jury that now began to scrutinize Johnson's life. On October 12, the government men took Lucille from her guarded hotel room to give testimony, hoping that the girl would say Jack had abducted her from Minneapolis. Mrs. Alice Phillips Aldrich of the Law and Order League had been granted access to Lucille and had labored to convince her that she ought to incriminate Johnson. They were all concentrating on the matter of the supposed abduction, and crossing state lines, as this would be a violation of the Mann Act and likely to bring Jack to a Federal penitentiary. The fact that Johnson was not guilty of abduction not only meant nothing to these people, it was clear outside their range of perception. They were obsessed with the notion that Johnson was such a bad man that it was their duty to destroy him by hook or by crook. They thought they were in the position of sanitary engineers called upon to remove a nuisance from the street—it made no difference how they went about it, so long as they took the offensive thing away. But to their great annoyance and frustration, Lucille refused to incriminate Johnson; after two hours of questioning, she collapsed from the strain and they took her away—this time to jail.

Nobody could say Jack's lawyers had given Lucille any instructions. Attorney Robert E. Cantwell, appearing for Jack, had failed both in proffering the bail money, and in obtaining a writ of habeas corpus, being repulsed on the latter plea before Judge George A. Carpenter, and also

before Judge Kennesaw Mountain Landis, who was later
to become notorious for the ferocity of the punishments
he inflicted on bootleggers. Waiting outside the jury room,
Cantwell asked if he might interview the girl.

"No, you cannot see her," said Assistant U. S. District
Attorney Harry A. Parkin. "And that isn't all—you will
not get to see her."

Mrs. Cameron-Falconet appeared at the Federal Building with Charley Erbstein. The lawyer was in a good
mood. He said, "I feel that Jack Johnson has insulted every
white woman in the United States. I want to see justice
done."

It may seem as we study this matter today that these
people were on extremely high horses where Johnson was
concerned; we should therefore keep constantly in mind
the emotional and political climate in which these events
were taking place. Erbstein, Parkin, Mrs. Cameron-
Falconet, Arthur Farwell, the Federal vice detectives, the
jurors—these were merely members of the posse comitatus
hunting Johnson down. Never did a posse ride out with
firmer public backing; so far as anyone could tell, the entire nation had agreed to the necessity of official moral
reform, and in the Middle West Johnson personified everything that ought to be suppressed by law. So in considering
Erbstein, for example, we will find him not only a belligerent lawyer of a familiar type, but also a resident of Chicago who was aware that the governing body of the city
itself had condemned Jack Johnson.

This unheard-of municipal procedure had been carried
out the day before Lucille's grand jury examination, when
a specially convened night session of the City Council

passed a resolution denouncing Johnson and urging the revocation of his café license. What made the scene all the more amazing was the presence of a crowd that packed the galleries and frequently interrupted the reading of the resolution with applause. At least one citizen of neighboring St. Louis would have liked to join in the applause with the Chicagoans. Mr. J. B. Cummings, a man of mark and president of the Missouri Central Telephone and Electric Light Company, wrote as follows to Cook County Civil Service Commissioner Frederic Greer: "Dear Fred: If Chicago men let Jack Johnson get away with the insult to all white women—that he can get any one he wants— Then here's hoping that Chicago gets wiped off the map."

Reading the papers in the closing weeks of October, 1912, one would suppose that it was Johnson, and not officials of the U. S. government, who held Lucille prisoner. She was still in jail, and Mrs. Aldrich continued to point out the error of her ways. In spite of it all, Lucille held to her determination not to return to Minneapolis. Nor would she agree to end her association—whatever it was—with Johnson. Though it increased the pressure of public indignation, this loyalty must have warmed Johnson's heart, for one member of his family seemed to have turned against him: his brother Charles was reported as saying he thought Jack should be sent to prison. Moreover, Charles was giving the grand jury "important evidence." Charles' opinion was backed by the young members of the Christian Endeavor League of the Bethel African Methodist Episcopal Church, who said Jack was a bad citizen. They would not condone his "breaking the law of the land."

Just what law Johnson violated in conducting a licensed saloon and appearing before the public as an entertainer and professional boxer was not made clear by his black and white detractors. In truth, the government lawyers were sitting up nights trying to put together an indictment that could be taken seriously. They knew there was nothing in the abduction charge, no matter what Erbstein said. Disorderly conduct they could prove with no trouble; but after the miles of newsprint, and the tumult, and the hurrying to and fro, and the resolutions in city council, this would be an absurd result, a ridiculous mouse born of a preposterously laboring bureaucratic mountain. They kept digging, and, meanwhile, city detectives were posted at the Café de Champion "to prevent trouble."

Now there appeared in court a Negro named Willard Davis, who entered suit against Johnson for alienating the affections of his wife, Adah Banks Davis. She was the woman who had shot Johnson because of Lucille. Like the abduction charge, this accusation never came to trial; it served only to show that Jack was now a public target, like the Negro or black-up white on the midway of a county fair, a mark for anyone who wanted to throw a baseball at his head.

On November 1, the State of Illinois canceled the liquor license under which Johnson was doing business and closed the Café de Champion. The bartenders, waiters, and piano-pounders scuttled off, impelled by fear of the police and a sure instinct that the place would never open again. They were right. The brewery that had backed Johnson made no effort to resume business at that address. The building was torn down, and a neatly kept lawn enclosed by a cyclone fence now occupies the site. The lawn sets off the research center of the Association of American Railroads on the campus of the Illinois Institute of Technology.

Next morning the *Inter-Ocean* reported the closing in a news story that sounded like the work of an editorial writer. The opening sentences set the tone: "Chicago has written finis to the career of Jack Johnson, Negro pugilist. He will not be allowed to violate the laws any longer." Meanwhile, the Federal men working to jail Johnson suddenly began to display smiles in the corridors of the court house, and to stand each other drinks at Henrici's—they had found a witness to testify that Johnson was guilty of transporting a woman across state lines for immoral purposes, thus violating the Mann Act. The witness was the woman herself—Belle Schreiber. At this point letters arrived from George Thomas, an American promoter in the capital of Czarist Russia. Thomas offered to arrange for Johnson to fight Sam Langford in St. Petersburg, and promised music hall bookings throughout Russia, whose inhabitants were as curious then as they are today about anything from America. Sig Hart advised Johnson to catch the first train for New York, and the first boat for Europe; but Jack said he would not leave Chicago while Lucille was deprived of liberty. At the moment, this was taken as an especially sinister remark, but from our vantage point in time, it may be interpreted differently—even to the extent of showing that there were occasions when Johnson could be something astonishingly like a gentleman.

The chivalrous gesture served only to bring more trouble to Jack. On November 7, the blow fell in the form of a

Federal grand jury returned before Judge Landis and charging a violation of the Mann Act with Belle Schreiber. It was observed that none of this related to Lucille, whose mother had started the hue and cry. However, a force of detectives strong enough to take the most desperate kidnapper went to the Café de Champion, seized Johnson, and put handcuffs on him. He wept when he saw the shackles; but Attorney Edwin C. Day immediately laid memoranda showing ownership of property worth $30,000 before Judge Landis, and Johnson was released on bail.

Next day the matter of bail received further consideration, and after several hours of argument, Landis decided to reject the property he had accepted the day before. He also began to get angry, and twitch upon the woolsack. Lawyer Day offered to raise $30,000 in cash, and Landis said, "I will not accept a cash bond in this case. There is a human cry in this case that cannot be overlooked in consideration of a bond."

The police again seized Johnson, and took him to the city jail, where a swarm of press photographers closed in. Jack's arms were shackled, but he landed a fairly good kick on one of the pressmen, and the fellow limped away whining. The warders put Jack in a cell by himself, and he called for candles and wine, like the highwayman brought to Newgate. They filled only the first part of his order, and Johnson went to bed, taking off his own shoes for the first time since Reno.

Johnson had good lawyers; next morning the respected Benjamin Bachrach appeared before Judge Carpenter asking for a writ of habeas corpus to get Johnson out of jail. He attacked the constitutionality of the Mann Act, pointing out that it violated the Tenth Amendment; and he argued that Johnson was being held in violation of the Fifth Amendment. Carpenter threw him out of court; both Lucille and Jack now lay under lock and key.

Four days later, word spread through Chicago that there would be additional charges against Johnson. In fact, the indictment had contained these items from the start, but the Federal agents had hesitated to release the full text because of the affront to public decency in some of the charges. Indecency there was, to be sure—as much in the hunting out of the details as in what they signified. The historian now confronts the task of getting this matter into a plain record without compounding the offensiveness. It should suffice to say that Belle Schreiber would on occasion follow certain courses of action that are part of any career prostitute's repertoire; the Federal men had inquired about this, and got Belle to state that Johnson had participated in such acts, and they included the charges in the indictment. It had eleven counts, some of which seem redundant to the non-legal eye, charging in sum that Johnson brought Belle from Pittsburgh to Chicago on October 15, 1910, for the purposes of: (1) prostitution; (2) debauchery; (3) prostitution; (4) debauchery; (5) unlawful sexual intercourse; (6) committing the crime against nature; (7) prostitution; (8) unlawful sexual intercourse; (9) to induce prostitution; (10) unlawful sexual intercourse, and (11) crime against nature. For all its bumbling, this repetitious document struck the Federal men as a fine piece of legal draftsmanship. To them it was something on the order of a shotgun load, of which any pellet would bring down the bird.

Mayor Carter Harrison, Jr. now stepped to the center of the stage. He announced that his police had "clamped down" on the entire Levee district, and that not a brothel, low dance hall, or questionable saloon remained in operation. It was true. Chicago detectives stood watching in the railroad stations as hundreds of pimps, whores, and drug peddlers stowed themselves aboard the outgoing trains. Also in the caravan were large numbers of the lush workers who for years had harvested the wallets of the drunks who staggered from Levee saloons, and the mouse workers who terrorized and robbed homosexuals. The police had not bothered any respectable pickpockets or burglars, and the skilled confidence men and package thieves who worked the Loop hotels were also left undisturbed. But commercialized vice with its by-products, as an industry characterizing one neighborhood, was finished in Chicago. "That district is closed forever," said the mayor, and he was right.

After Johnson had spent four days in prison, Judge Landis cooled down enough to admit him to bail under the guarantee of $32,000 worth of property offered by his mother. Jack emerged into a much quieter atmosphere than that of the days when the excitement about Lucille had been at its height; the parades, the speeches by Farwell and the eloquent ministers in his movement, the last flauntings of the Levee people—these had raised public emotion to an intolerable pitch, and the city's nervous system was bound to relax. Shaken by his imprisonment, Johnson was in a mood to listen to his lawyers and to his Negro friends, all of whom begged him to lie low. He did so, and nothing was heard about Jack and his affairs for ten days; then it was Lucille who brought herself and Johnson back to public attention. We have seen that after Lucille's appearance before the grand jury, the Federal men threw her into jail. The place of captivity was the county prison at the nearby town of Rockford, where the government agents thought Lucille would soften up and become amenable to their demands that she testify against Johnson. When the Schreiber material came in, they no longer needed Lucille, and quietly released her early on the morning of Monday, November 25. Lucille went to Chicago with her mother and they put up at the same hotel where she had previously been detained. On the second day, she went out to visit a dressmaker and did not return. Mrs. Cameron-Falconet received a letter in the next day's mail that said, "I shall send you my permanent address later. I am away out in the West and intend to remain there." The envelope had a Chicago postmark.

One week later, Jack Johnson and Lucille Cameron were married at the Wabash Avenue house. Two Negro ministers performed the ceremony and Fred Danielson, a white saloonkeeper, was best man. After the ceremony a band struck up for dancing, and caterers began opening champagne. A number of reporters were there, and one of them asked Lucille, "Where's your mother, Mrs. Johnson?" "I don't know and I don't care," said the bride. Johnson's mother was present but replied when asked for a statement, "Sometimes I say things Jack doesn't like, so I'll keep my thoughts to myself." As the corks popped, Johnson took the "$2,500 ring" from his wife's finger and put it in his pocket.

Johnson legally married was somewhat harder to vilify

and condemn than Johnson the alleged abductor. As had
been the case with Etta, his marriage presented his detractors with a worrisome paradox: it legitimized a relationship that should never have been started in the first
place, as they saw it. Thus it drew attention away from
Johnson as an individual, and into the area where the
general question of inter-racial marriage was up for debate. Another effect of the marriage was to start a legend
that gained credence as to be taken for basic undeniable
fact; this was the notion that Johnson had married Lucille
so that, as his wife, she could not be compelled to testify
against him when he came to trial. This was printed as an
item of common knowledge in most of Johnson's obit-
uaries. The idea is neat and plausible, and fits with the
conception of Johnson as a man of great low cunning. The
only thing wrong with it is its complete untruth; we have
seen that the indictment had nothing to do with Lucille,
and so far as testifying goes, we also have seen that the
Federal men with all their pressure could not get her to
say a word against Jack.

For about a week after the wedding, many people condemned Johnson as severely for the actual marriage as
they had for the supposed abduction. One quotation will
serve to sum up the fury: on the floor of Congress, Representative Rodenberry of Georgia said that "in Chicago,
white girls are made the slaves of an African brute." Most
of Johnson's critics, like the Congressman, were too angry
to give the marriage a cool examination. Those who were
able to do so concluded that Johnson brought several bad
factors to the marriage in addition to the inter-racial aspect
with its automatic social handicaps and difficulties. There

was the matter of Etta, not yet three months in her grave; there was the probability that he had been unfaithful to Etta and that this at least would be established as fact at the trial; and there was the problem of his habits of life, with drinking and gambling, and the day bound to come when he would no longer be champion and would have to face the world barred from the liquor business, and not likely to catch on as athletic trainer at any reputable college or club. Leaving the color of either partner aside, Johnson was about the worst matrimonial prospect in the world for a young girl. It should be noticed, therefore, that the marriage lasted twelve years, and in comparison with the average show-business marriage of the present day, Jack and Lucille look like Mr. and Mrs. John Anderson as immortalized by Robert Burns.

Looking back on the widespread discussion of Jack Johnson at this time, the emphasis on his color might lead one to suppose that the entire white population was in arms against the country's Negroes. This was far from the case. In many parts of the country, white men and women were trying to clear the way for Negroes to rise into a better life. To this end they tried to open not only the doors of material opportunity through which Booker Washington hoped his people would enter the main stream of American achievement, but the doors of social equality as well. To give an example in Chicago, and shortly after Johnson and Lucille were married, we need only contemplate the action of the League of Cook County Women's Clubs in canceling a luncheon at the Hotel La Salle when the management refused to serve the Negro members. More than one thousand white women walked out of the hotel, refusing to listen to the manager's plea that public opinion would not permit him to entertain colored guests. It would seem that the hotel man was in direct contact with a demonstration that public opinion among progressive people in Cook County at least held just the opposite view. And let us note that these clubwomen, making their gesture toward the racial integration of public facilities, were also one of the strongest elements in the movement for moral reform.

This movement was rising to its crest; nothing relating to it now could be too far-fetched for respectful attention, nothing too absurd to attain a prominent place in the newspapers. This was demonstrated a few days after the La Salle lost the women's luncheon, when an official of the Young Men's Christian Association detected a bad influence in a dignified institution on Michigan Avenue. As an international secretary of the Y.M.C.A., E. J. Elliott had studied manners and customs throughout the world, but it shocked him to see men at the University Club "spending their time on cards and tobacco." He had entered the building as a guest, and upon emerging gave a statement to reporters. "I consider the University Club a curse," said Elliott. "During my visit, I was put face to face with men who were smoking and gambling." Mr. Elliott was far from a fool; he knew the clubmen were among the most substantial and conservative citizens of Chicago. That such men could seem to him to be supporters of organized evil gives some idea of the character in which Jack Johnson would appear when the day came to answer the government's charges in court.

It will be noticed that E. J. Elliott failed to indict the

highball drinkers of the University Club. This should not
be taken as evidence that liquor dealers were having an
easy time. Although the onslaught of Mayor Harrison's
police had destroyed the business of prostitution, thousands of licensees were still trying to conduct saloons in
areas where brothel-keepers had been their neighbors,
and in many cases their colleagues. City police and agents
of the Illinois Vice Commission and the Committee of
Fifteen now began to make life miserable for these small
tavern operators. The officers arrested the saloon men on
every conceivable variety of four basic charges: that they
sold drink to intoxicated persons; that they permitted disorderly conduct; that they sold liquor on Sunday; and that
they allowed a mysterious offense known as "loitering with
intent." Times were hard indeed for the free-lance prostitutes who had never been inmates of the recognized
houses, but had cruised around the taprooms picking up
clients at random; and there was hardship among the
bartenders who had been accustomed to eke out their
wages with the modest sums they could earn as agents for
these women.

The date of Johnson's trial was set for the middle of
May, and he began to hold long conferences with his
attorneys. They told him that he need not worry about
the counts of the indictment having to do with specific
actions: his denial would have the same weight as Belle
Schreiber's accusation. But it would not be so easy to deal
with the matter of violating the Mann Act by transporting
the woman across state lines. Here they were going to
challenge the constitutionality of the Act itself, but they
told Johnson not to count on this argument winning him

free; many able lawyers had attacked the legislation on these grounds and had seen their clients go to prison. Perhaps Johnson read a dispatch in the *Inter-Ocean* at about this time that gave severe point to the attorneys' warning: Mann Act convictions had crowded Federal prisons beyond capacity. The government penitentiaries at Leavenworth and Atlanta were so uncomfortably full, the report stated, that inmates were being transferred to state prisons. During the year 1912, Federal judges had handed down more prison sentences for violating the Mann Act than in any previous *ten* years for smuggling and counterfeiting.

Such were the discouraging circumstances under which Jack Johnson at last went to trial, on May 13, 1913, before a jury and Judge George Albert Carpenter. Though no mental giant, Carpenter was a superior type of man as Federal judges go. A native Chicagoan, he had married an Isham, and lived in one of that family's handsome town houses on the near North Side. His brother was the composer John Alden Carpenter, later to write the music for the "Krazy Kat Ballet," which was based on a comic strip.

Johnson took the stand in his own defense. He admitted many things, such as having sent Belle Schreiber money at various times; in fact, the total came to between nine and ten thousand dollars, but no remittance had been made with immoral purposes in view. He spoke in a low voice, at times with noticeable hesitation. Sweat stood on his forehead and trickled down the sides of his face. Once or twice he attempted the appealing smile that Arthur Ruhl had seen at Reno. Nobody smiled back: his own lawyers looked anxious, and the faces of the prosecutors and jury were purposeful and stern. Using the nothing-to-hide technique, Lawyer Bachrach asked, "Did you have a conversation with Belle Schreiber over the telephone in October, 1910?"

"Yes," said Johnson, "she called me up and asked me to send her seventy-five dollars."

"Did you?"

"Yes."

"At this time did you send her a telegram telling her to come to Chicago and to wait for you here?"

"I don't think I did."

Here Judge Carpenter interrupted to ask Jack to state whether or not he was certain about the telegram. Johnson then said he was positive he had never sent the message. He added that he could not say whether or not his associates had sent one without his knowledge.

"When you sent the seventy-five dollars," Bachrach went on, "did you have any intention who should come here for immoral purposes, collectively or individually?"

"No, I did not."

"When you came to Chicago about this time, did you come here to see Belle?"

"No. I came on arrangements about some boxing."

"Did you hunt her up?"

"No. She called me on the telephone. She wanted me to fix up a flat for her and her sister and mother to live in. I spent about a thousand dollars in fixing up her flat, and then gave her five hundred in cash to keep her going until she could get a job as a stenographer."

On cross-examination, Federal Attorney Parkin tried to

show that Johnson had given money and furniture to Belle as an investment rather than as a gift to a valued friend. The prosecutor cried, "Didn't you forcibly take twenty dollars from Belle Schreiber which she had earned immorally?"

"No," said Johnson, "I never took a dollar, a cent, or even a newspaper from her. What would I want with twenty dollars when I was earning twenty-five hundred a week?"

Belle Schreiber's testimony was a chronicle of trips around the country and into Canada in Johnson's company. She spoke of sums paid for traveling expenses, and for hotel suites at Oakland and San Francisco. As Belle told it, her life sounded dreary: "I was driven out of disreputable houses in Pittsburgh, Cleveland, and other cities. They didn't want me because I was Jack Johnson's white sweetheart. Bad as the places were, I was too bad to remain in them."

With sympathy in his voice, Bachrach asked, "Did you love Jack?" Belle replied, "I don't believe I did. I don't believe I ever knew what love was."

Court had convened at ten o'clock in the morning, and the prosecution and defense ended their cases by ten o'clock that night. As Bachrach predicted, the Federal men abandoned the charges relating to specific acts, and rested on the accusations of interstate travel with improper intent. Bachrach told the jury that the Mann Act was faulty legislation; and even so, there was "not a scintilla of evidence" that Jack had violated it. In his turn, Parkin made an emotional appeal. He said, "If you should find the defendant not guilty, knowing as you do the evidence in the case, I do not see how you could ever look squarely in the faces of those persons whom you respect and admire, and especially how you could ever look squarely into the faces of your mothers, wives, and daughters." From Johnson's point of view, the most hopeful passage in Judge Carpenter's remarks to the jurymen was, "The court instructs the jury that a colored man has equal rights with a white man under the law. The courts protect him. A verdict should be rendered as if the defendant were a man of your own color."

The jurymen were out for an hour and forty-five minutes, coming in at a quarter to midnight. Judge Carpenter was called from his chambers, and Johnson from the corridor where he had been pacing up and down. When called on to announce the verdict, the foreman's answer showed that the jury had listened attentively to Judge Carpenter's charge. A colored man had just as much right to be convicted under the Mann Act as a white man—and they had convicted Johnson.

Judge Carpenter set June 4 as the day he would pronounce sentence, and continued Johnson in the same bail. As Johnson and Bachrach walked down the hall outside the courtroom, a reporter called out, "What do you think of it, Jack?" Johnson answered, "I haven't a thing to say—not a thing. My attorney will answer for me." Bachrach then said, "I can't account for the verdict. It was a very hard case."

That the hard case would bring a harsh sentence seemed inevitable; yet his friends reported that Johnson with his ingrained optimism could not accept the idea that he might go to prison. While waiting to learn his fate, he might have taken comfort from the tolerant viewpoint expressed by a Chicago pastor in choosing a boxing ring for a pulpit as a means of underlining his message that "we are all engaged in a fight in life." Perhaps this sort of evangelizing might create sympathy for Johnson's struggle to rise in the world; but the general condemnation of immoral life outweighed it, and the voices of such mighty churchmen as the Bishop of Bombay, who cried that thousands of Indian women were disappearing every year, presumably into the clutches of vice lords, were heard by a larger audience than that of the Chicago pastor. The underworld took its cue from the great men: as the last week before the day of judgment went by, the papers reported that no professional gambler in Chicago would bet that Johnson was not going to jail.

At sentencing time, Judge Carpenter opened the proceedings by denying Bachrach's motion for a new trial; then he delivered a few cold remarks: "It is always an unpleasant duty for me to say what will compensate the government for violating its laws. The crime which this defendant stands convicted of is an aggravating one. The life of the defendant, by his own admission, had been such as to merit condemnation. We have had a number of defendants found guilty in this court of violations of the Mann Act who have been sentenced to severe punishment, from one to two years in the penitentiary. This defendant is one of the best known men of his race, and his example has been far-reaching, and the court is bound to consider the position he occupied among his people. In view of these facts, this is a case that calls for more than a fine."

Carpenter thereupon sentenced Johnson to one year and one day in the Joliet penitentiary, plus a fine of $1,000. He then granted two weeks' stay of execution to give Bachrach time to make his formal try at getting the conviction reversed in the Circuit Court of Appeals. During these fourteen days, Johnson would remain free under the bond he had given at the time of the indictment.

V
Flight

Nothing would ever convince Johnson that the sentence had not been dictated by racial prejudice. The hundreds of white people in jail on similar charges meant nothing to him. What stuck in his mind was Carpenter's remark about being one of the best known men of his race; as Johnson saw it, this was the same as an affidavit that he would not have been sentenced to prison if his skin had been white. As we look at this episode today, it appears that *any* keeper of a low saloon, notorious in morals, marrying a young girl over her mother's objection so soon after his wife's self-destruction in sordid circumstances, and convicted of carrying a prostitute around the country would be fined and sent to jail by a man of Carpenter's background. But even if race had nothing to do with it, the sentence was severe, for the fine of $1,000 would have been only a tiny part of Johnson's financial loss. A year out of action now that his earning power was at its height would cost him about a quarter of a million. That was too much: Johnson began to make plans to jump bail.

A thought that he might try this very thing had entered the minds of the Federal men, and with the aid of city detectives they shadowed Johnson day and night. They also kept watch on his friends and family; nevertheless, Lucille was able to slip out of town without being observed. She went to Canada, and took discreet lodgings in Montreal. The following day Johnson drove all over Chicago in his red touring car, trailed by the police. Everything depended on his giving them the slip, and he managed it by suddenly wrenching the wheel and turning up an alley. There he jumped into a waiting automobile piloted by Gus Rhodes, and they hurried to the railroad station at Forty-second Street on the South Side. Their plan was to exploit Johnson's resemblance to Rube Foster, whose team was leaving for the East that day. The thing was closely timed—the train was in motion when Johnson and Gus came running up the iron stairway with their arms full of baseball equipment. They believed that any police who had the station under surveillance would mistake Jack for Rube; whether or not police were there, Johnson got out of Chicago on this train without interference.

The next part of the escape also worked perfectly. It was quite simple: before reaching Buffalo, the train ran into Canada, making a stop at Hamilton, Ontario; here Johnson and Rhodes stepped off. Canadian police arrested Jack almost at once; but he had been aware that he might be taken in on sight, and had with him the names of two Hamilton lawyers who could be called on for fast consultation. These attorneys accompanied Johnson before a justice of the peace and obtained his freedom on the ground that there was no official demand for his return to the United States. This was true, the reason being that the authorities in Chicago did not yet know he had left town. As Johnson recalled afterward, "That j.p. never had a chance. Those lawyers just talked me loose." Gus and Jack did not linger over congratulations, but hastened on to Montreal and met Lucille. She had booked steamship tickets, and on July 1 the three of them sailed on board the *Carinthia*, bound for Le Havre.

"Well, the cable's cut," said Johnson, as the liner put out to sea. "We're the three musketeers!" cried Lucille. A year before, she had been a schoolgirl in Minneapolis. A few months before, she had been in jail. And now with the Canadian coastline fading in the west, and the mystery of Europe looming ahead, she felt that her situation was the essence of romance. The other passengers, however, took a harsh and realistic view of the Johnson party. Gloomily surveying a tip he feared would be taken back, the chief steward carried out the purser's order and told Johnson that there might be "some difficulty about the seatings in the dining saloon." Jack was tired of dissension, and said that he and his companions would prefer to be served in their staterooms.

Needless to say, Johnson's flight caused a worldwide sensation; and in Chicago his prosecutors raved and cursed when they heard he had eluded them. There were scenes of recrimination between Federal men and city officials, made all the more bitter by the rumor that Johnson had paid $10,000 to politicians for arranging his escape. The basis of this story was that Johnson had learned from underworld sources that "everything could be fixed for ten thousand dollars." On looking into the matter, Jack had decided the politicians could not deliver the goods.

Judge Carpenter was not very bright, but he was honest, and Johnson knew it; the suggestion that outside forces could arrange an illegal settlement was nothing more than an attempt to steal Jack's money. But this was small comfort to the prosecutors, who took Johnson's departure as an insult, and talked about it in the tone of angry men. Assistant U. S. Attorney Elwood Goodman showed how they felt when he heard that the other passengers objected to Johnson's presence on the ship. "This may solve the whole problem," he said. "The passengers may mutiny and heave him away on an iceberg."

Johnson knew how to shrug off such talk, but when the voyage ended he found it alarming to look out at Le Havre and see a detachment of French police drawn up on the pier. It was a relief to learn they were not there to arrest him, but to control the crowds that came to stare as he disembarked. He was now more than the heavyweight champion: he was also the world's most notorious fugitive from justice. In this double character, Johnson was to be an object of intense curiosity wherever he went; often enough, he would mistake morbid interest for approbation, an error that would lead to trouble. He was to live for a considerable time in an ambivalent relation to his audience. He had defied public opinion in about as many ways as it was possible for one man to do it; yet it would have been an irretrievable disaster for Johnson if the public had turned completely away from him. He had to have a paying audience, even if it came to hoot and jeer.

This part of Johnson's life began with a brief stay in Paris. Attending the Folies Bergère with Gus and Lucille, he was spotlighted in the audience and called to the stage amid applause to shake hands with the stars of the entertainment. Here Jack was in the friendliest possible atmosphere, but somehow he got the notion that he would do better as a music hall attraction in England. The three musketeers accordingly set out for London late in August. Johnson got into a street fight shortly before their departure, but the two events had no connection. Johnson had objected to an insult to Lucille in front of a café, and the crowd took sides about the matter; there was pushing, a blow, a fight between two Frenchmen, then a general mêlée. Caught by the hurly-burly, Johnson landed several punches in self-defense; then the police came whirling their lead-weighted billies, stopped the disturbance, exonerated Jack and sent him on his way. In describing the affair to Gus Rhodes, Johnson shook his head in wonder at the expert manner in which Frenchmen kicked each other during the brawl. His astonishment at this method of combat was to be shared a few years later by his compatriots in the American Expeditionary Force, as they recorded in the song "Mademoiselle from Armetières."

Though Johnson was not responsible for the street fight in Paris, the London newspapers tried to discourage him from booking his act in British music halls. Two years before, after the shock of the Jeffries fight had worn off, the *Times* had said a few kind words about Johnson: "He sported rather more gold teeth than are worn by gentlemen in the Shires, and enough diamonds to resemble a starry night, but he was on the whole a far more pleasant person to meet in a room than any of the white champions of complicated nationality whom America exports from

time to time to these unwilling shores." The reference to
complicated nationality was aimed at Tommy Burns. As
we have noted, Burns became unpopular when he called
the British champion a bum and knocked him unconscious
in the ring. By contrast, Johnson might be taken as an
amusing, exotic sort of fellow, except that the British
now were saturated with white slave agitation arising
from the Chicago trial. Did Johnson abduct women, and
keep them locked up, and take money they earned by
degradation? It made no difference that he had never
done any of these things, and was obviously not doing
them at the present time. He *was* fleeing from the sentence
handed down in a court of law. With this as their cue, the
British papers went into long speeches that could be
boiled down to six words: *Jack Johnson is not welcome
here*.

By August 20, it was evident that in addition to the
newspaper disapproval of Johnson, a barrier to his appearance in England was being erected by his theatrical
colleagues. These were the members of the Variety
Artists' Federation, who reacted with "astonishment and
resentment" at the news that a syndicate headed by
Frederic Tozer had engaged Johnson to perform in halls
in London and the provinces on a tour for which they
would pay him £1,000 per week. His first appearances
would be at the Euston and South London variety theaters, where the greatest acts played to the most knowing
audiences. The rank and file of Federation members
called this a desecration of the music hall as an artistic
medium. We might bear in mind that most of these people
were pitiably lacking in talent, and barely earned a living

with their moth-eaten costumes, feeble dances, and vapid songs. All they had was the conviction that they were entitled to be called artists. The *Times* reporter wrote, "There is a general desire to make it clear that this is not a question of color. It is a question of maintaining the standard of music-hall art. That Jack Johnson should appear on the stage of a London music-hall is regarded as unthinkable, and those who hold that view do so without in any way wishing to prejudice any issue which may be pending or decided in America concerning the pugilist."

No doubt this was very high-minded; at that period in England's history, there was no clean-cut distinction between considerations of morals and questions of taste. Yet a little while, and there would fall on England a catastrophe so enormous and terrible that it could not be imagined. But now as Johnson prepared to visit the country, the upper middle class that ruled seemed to be engrossed in matters of no more importance than the disappointing grouse season—though good bags had been taken on Auchintorlie Moor in Dumbartonshire—and a problem that was debated in the *Times* under the heading, "Changing Conventions in the Ball-Room." Here Johnson's name got into the discussion. A writer to the *Times* deplored the dances known as the Turkey Trot and the Bunny Hug, and stated that the police in Washington, D. C., had forbidden their performance in the streets "by the little colored 'chillen.'" Now that Jack Johnson was in England, the writer went on, we would doubtless see more of these abominable dances.

That sort of suspicion—the feeling that Johnson was up to no good, no matter if what he appeared to be doing was harmless—now inspired a professional reformer to oppose him. As secretary of both the National Vigilance Association and the International Bureau for the Suppression of the White Slave Traffic, W. A. Coote had authority of a kind, and when he called for a public demonstration against Johnson's so much as putting a foot on British soil, Frederic Tozer and his colleagues groaned in anguish. They could see pounds, shillings, and pence flying away like the grouse who had deserted their usual grounds and spoiled the sport; and the only defense they could think of was to talk about "British fair play," to mutter that the feeling against Johnson was caused by "American prejudice," and to state that "We quite agree with the Artists' Federation that notoriety only should not suffice in the engagement of 'turns.' Jack Johnson is an able exponent of muscular prowess, and also an amusing entertainer."

The exponent of muscular prowess landed at Folkestone on August 24. The crowd was large, and neither friendly nor hostile; Albert Jenkins of the Tozer office appeared to help Jack and his two companions through customs, then ushered them to a hired touring car for the drive to London. They got there early in the afternoon, and Johnson issued a statement: "I am surprised at the attitude of my fellow artists, with whom I have previously been on excellent terms of friendship. In England you speak of the White Slave Act and people naturally are shocked, but when they speak of White Slave laws in the States, they mean something very different to what you have here, and there is really no need for any good clergyman to squirm about it."

Johnson was referring to a certain Rev. F. B. Meyer, a

dissenting minister who had been noticeably wrought up about the proposed English tour. To make sure Meyer got the point, Jack wrote him a letter: "Dear Sir, As a visitor to London, I have seen by several papers your own view regarding my character and so forth. I would like, Sir, very much for you to come and have an audience with me for one half hour—namely, Wednesday afternoon, at 4 o'clock. I shall ask the Press to be present. Yours truly, Champion Jack Arthur Johnson." There was no reply.

Tozer and Jenkins decided to introduce Johnson on the following night from a box at the Euston Theater of Varieties, so they could say he was merely a member of the audience if things got out of hand. Accordingly, Jack sat resplendent in white tie and tails as two wretched female performers, who had been among the strongest objectors to his appearance, tried to get through their acts. There was a long-standing tradition of toleration for rowdies in the galleries of music halls, and Johnson seemed to have enthusiastic supporters among these ruffians. They made such an uproar that the women who had been critical of Johnson were compelled to walk off without finishing their songs. The master of ceremonies then called Johnson to the stage. There was loud and fairly prolonged applause, with cries of dissent here and there. Johnson raised his clenched fists and cried, "Thank you—thank you very much. My real crime—my real crime—was beating Jim Jeffries!" This pleased the crowd, and Johnson left the stage to more applause. Tozer felt better about the tour's chances of eventual success, but agreed with Jenkins that they had better proceed with extreme caution so far as metropolitan bookings were concerned. There had been

an ugly tone in Johnson's gallery support that told these
experienced managers it could easily turn against him;
and in any event, no music hall owner wanted a riot on his
hands. With Johnson's concurrence, Tozer thereupon
called the newspapermen to his office the following afternoon, promising an important announcement. As we know,
Johnson had been getting a bad press; one reason was that
in those days British reporters were very poorly paid, and
they envied and resented Johnson's jewelry and fine
clothes. Tozer now hoped to win them over by frankness,
but those who came to his office showed undissembled
incredulity as he said, "In the matter of his fitness to appear in the music halls, Jack Johnson is arranging interviews and taking other measures to meet the allegations.
In the meantime, concurring with the view of the management that for the present his appearances as arranged
would be inadvisable, he has requested the postponement
of his London engagement. This does not affect the provincial engagements including Birmingham, Manchester,
Edinburgh, and Leeds."

In spite of Tozer's bland optimism, he was not able to
provide Johnson with consecutive bookings, though Jack
earned more than eight thousand pounds for the appearances that could be made. Public acceptance of Johnson
was spotty, like the grouse season—sometimes good, sometimes not so good. Late in August, the *Times* grouse correspondent reported the largest bag of the season when
Mr. H. R. Rimington-Wilson's party of nine guns took
1,320 brace on Broomhead Moor. This proved to be an
augury for Jack: within a week, he was playing to a full
house and standees at the Rosherville Gardens in Graves-

end Bay. But again the luck changed: on the following day, his car collided with a taxicab in the Wilton Road near Victoria Station. Johnson used the excuse that he had sprained his back in the accident to cancel an appearance scheduled for Hull, where the feeling against Jack appeared to be intense; the theater manager told Tozer's advance men he feared the seats would be torn out.

Johnson had no fear of hostile audiences, but he could understand the commercial disadvantages of outright rioting as well as any man. Discussing his prospects with Gus Rhodes, he decided his best course would be to return to the ring. They doubted that this could be done in England; they might find suitable opponents, but holding a big fight on British soil would depend on the National Sporting Club, where Johnson expected no consideration. And so, weighing one factor with another, he decided to resume his fighting career in France.

We may assume that Johnson's bank account was low when we consider that the first match he accepted in France was not in boxing, but in wrestling. Jack's opponent was a mountainous Russian named Al Spoul. In the bout, a succession of fouls caused bad feeling, and Johnson ended it by knocking Spoul unconscious. The record books list the affair under the heading of Johnson's victories by knockout, but it may be that this was a staged spectacle with a faked blow as the climax. But no matter what the circumstances, it was a sad thing for Johnson with his grace and skill to be involved in such a performance.

Jack's great need at this time, as it had been when he dealt with Jim Jeffries, was a competent promoter. And in November it appeared that he had met such a man in

9. Jack and the first of his three white wives, Etta Duryea, at the Paris races.

10. Christmas day at Jack Johnson's home. Jack embraces his mother and wife Lucille. George Little at left.

11. Johnson arriving at Bow St. Police Court in answer to a summons for creating a disturbance and impeding traffic.

12. Jess Willard defeats Johnson in Havana, 1915: the famous "shaded eyes" photograph.

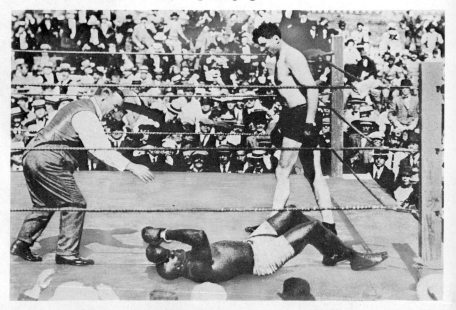

Dan McKetrick, an Irish-American who was staging fights in Paris under the corporate title of La Société pour la Propagation de la Boxe Française. McKetrick suggested that Johnson take on Francis Charles Moran, a red-haired young man from Pittsburgh who had served a hitch in the Navy. Moran had beaten good fighters and was feared for his devastating right swing, which was known as "the Old Mary Ann." Johnson was willing; the two boxers and the promoter signed contracts at a bottle-loaded table in the Bois de Boulogne. As McKetrick wanted plenty of time to build interest, the match would not take place until the following June.

With a championship match in France under what he took to be competent management assured, Jack came back to England in January, 1914. It seemed that the country had a fascination for him; but he met with opposition when he tried to book his music hall act at Hanley in North Staffordshire. Both the dissenting and official clergy were indignant at the thought of Johnson making an appearance in the parish, and the officers of the Territorials, their faces as scarlet as their tunics, refused the use of the Drill Hall. Tozer sent an agent to lease the Old Port Vale football ground, and the owners refused cash in hand. The *Times* said, "At present, Johnson has no place to go." In the same issue, the paper carried a discussion of the situation in professional boxing, with the conclusion that the heavyweight title was vacant. It also attacked Johnson for his "detestable trick of taunting an opponent." Johnson's inclination toward this appalling villainy did not prevent an outburst of interest in arranging a match between Jack and Sam Langford. The theatrical manager

C. B. Cochrane said he would put up a purse of £5,000 and find a suitable arena. Johnson was skeptical; he stayed in London while the Tozer office booked him into the Empire Theater at Wolverhampton, and then saw the engagement canceled because of pressure by the Rev. J. Davidson Brown, head of the local Free Church Council. Another booking was withdrawn when the Swansea Watch Committee threatened to take steps. It was hard to bear, for Johnson and his managers knew that unless he committed a breach of the peace, or performed on the stage in an indecent manner, there was nothing illegal about his theatrical activities. Jack reflected that here in the home of fair play for all, there were people who behaved remarkably like the reformers of Cook County.

And now the National Sporting Club was heard from. Cochrane's offer had vanished in a fog of publicity, as such things have a way of doing. But during the first week in February, the N.S.C. offered to guarantee Jack £3,000 to fight Langford. In disgust at what he regarded as too low an offer, Johnson returned to Paris. A few days later, the *Times* reported that "the tone which Jack Johnson has taken in communicating with the National Sporting Club is such as to preclude the possibility of his making a public reappearance in England." The letter that Johnson had written to the club from Paris was as follows:

"A. F. Bettinson, Esq., National Sporting Club, Covent Garden, London W. C. Dear Sir: I received your letter this morning and I must say that the offer which you have made to me is absolutely ridiculous to my thinking. I have defeated Langford, and not only that, Langford has been beaten four times in the last two years. He was beaten by Sam McVey in Australia; he was also defeated by Joe Jeannette on two different occasions in New York City, and not so long ago he was defeated by Gunboat Smith in his own home town, Boston, and the only thing I can get out of the fight is money, because there will be no glory in defeating Langford as I have already done the trick.

"And furthermore, the Club has gone so far as to make a match for me. They have also said there must be a £500 side bet, and they have dictated to me how much of the picture privilege I shall receive.

"I am very proud that I have made all my matches—I myself, and being a real champion I do not see where the National Sporting Club has a right to dictate to me how much I shall receive for my appearance and boxing ability. If they do not want to give my price—which is £6,000, win, lose or draw—then they don't need to wait until March 1st; they can call things off on receipt of this letter. I gave that to Burns—win, lose, or draw—I won my title on those conditions, and any time that I shall do battle it will be under those conditions and none other.

"I am a boxing man now, and I am getting my price. I don't care what the public thinks; I am the one to be satisfied. I have defeated every man before the public with the exception of two, and one of them is the man who beat Langford—Gunboat Smith. The other is Frank Moran, who is considered in America the superior of Gunboat Smith, and after my fight with Moran (which I feel sure to win) I am going to fight Gunboat Smith, and am also getting my price for that battle.

"Mr. C. B. Cochrane, of the Olympia, London, has

offered me £5,000. Why should I take £3,000? Yours truly, Jack Johnson, World's Heavyweight Champion."

Much of what Johnson said in his letter was true, but there also were troubles in Paris, where McKetrick was beset by worries and annoyances. He had the reputation of being high-strung and disputatious, and his temper was abraded by continual frustrations in his efforts to stage the Johnson-Moran fight. To begin with, McKetrick had distributed $3,600 in bribes among the French newspapermen, and expected some return on his money. Instead, the journalists raised a cry of *"Qui c'est, Moran?"* that was worse than disregarding the fight altogether. The promoter had to hand out additional gratuities, and hundreds of free tickets, which the reporters sold in competition with the box office, before they would consent to print his propaganda.

Another irritant was the conduct of Frank Moran, who made a trip to the United States just before the fight and came back with Ike Dorgan, Tad's brother, as his personal manager. McKetrick had reasons for wanting to continue as sole director of Moran's career. He called the boxer into conference.

"Let's you and I sign a contract, Frank," McKetrick said.

"I don't need no contract," Moran replied.

"Well, I do!" cried McKetrick, coming to a boil.

"I'm sorry, Dan," Moran said, "when I left the Navy, I took an oath never to sign no papers."

"You took an oath!" screamed McKetrick. "What if I take a punch at your head?"

"You've got more sense than that," said Moran, but McKetrick went away fuming. The truth is that the promoter was convinced Johnson was finished as a fighter, and that Moran would beat him, and then be worth "a fortune of money." McKetrick could not endure the thought of Ike Dorgan cutting in on this, and his fury and resentment grew to the point where he became a living illustration of the natural law that an Irishman who finally gives way to a grudge becomes an uncontrollable force. In this implacable mood, McKetrick vowed that nobody would get a sou of the gate receipts until he had things as he wanted them. Using as an excuse a claim for $1,497 paid to Moran for expenses, he instructed a French lawyer to tie up the funds in the box office the minute the bout was over, and not to pay either fighter until he gave the word.

In making this move, McKetrick was carried away by his rancor. But McKetrick was beyond argument; and he had all the more reason to believe Moran would be the next champion when Jack accepted a match with a Negro heavyweight named Jim Johnson, and broke a small bone in his left arm by the force of a blow to Jim's head. McKetrick also knew that Jack had not trained for Jim Johnson, and that his preparation for Moran was of the sketchiest sort—if indeed he was doing anything to get ready for the fight. Jack had installed Gus Rhodes and Lucille in a villa at Asnières, and claimed he went out for his road work so early in the morning that he was finished before other folks got up. He supported this story by saying he had seen an enormous number of soldiers moving along the road in the early dawns. Johnson did see these troops, but it was from his automobile, as he drove back to Asnières after closing the cabarets.

When the fight took place at the Vélodrome d'Hiver, McKetrick saw he had been mistaken about Moran's chances. It was true that Johnson was in poor condition, but his superlative defense held up; he avoided the old Mary Ann, and although his left arm was useless on the offense, he kept Moran in trouble. This displeased a unanimously anti-Johnson crowd that included Gaby Deslys, Mistinguett, Maurice Chevalier, the Dolly sisters, the Princesse de Polignac, and the novelist Elinor Glyn. Moran finally landed a punch, and the crowd went wild. Johnson politely stepped back and joined in the applause, pounding his gloved hands together and bowing to his opponent.

"My sincere congratulations, Frank," he said, flashing his golden smile. This was the detestable taunting that infuriated the London *Times*; even worse was the uppercut with which he then smashed Moran's nose. Throughout the fight, Johnson kept a preoccupied air, for he had heard rumors of writs and lawyers, and knew but too well what this could mean. As he feared, he was told after the fight that French police had grabbed the money and taken it away.

"Goodbye, money, you're going to be long gone," Johnson muttered, shaking his head, and drove to Asnières for a victory banquet of chicken, lobster, whiskey, and champagne, all obtained on credit. These events took place on the night of June 27, 1914. Next day in the provincial Bosnian town of Sarajevo, a political assassin shot the Austrian Archduke Francis Ferdinand. It was seen at once that this was one of those basic events around which mighty forces move; and the French soldiers Johnson had seen in the early mornings soon had reinforcements as the reserves answered the call. McKetrick's lawyer was among the reservists who took up arms, and in the excitement he left without giving his client the necessary papers to get the box office money from the Bank of France. When McKetrick cooled down and applied for the money, the bank officials told him they had no authority to release it. It had taken McKetrick four weeks to get into a mood to talk business with Dorgan and Moran, and by this time World War I had broken out; and so the settlement would have to wait until the lawyer got back to Paris on furlough. But the lawyer never got back: he was killed in one of the first engagements. And to this day not a sou of the gate receipts has ever been paid to anyone. McKetrick was still trying to get the money in 1927, enlisting the services of Mayor James J. Walker of New York City, who appealed in vain to the Bank of France while on a trip to Paris. So the Johnson-Moran fight must be cited as history's only world heavyweight championship fight in which the contestants worked without pay.

The only satisfaction Moran and Johnson ever got from this affair was that which they derived from an episode in 1918. In March of that year Moran's lawyer, a former boxing commissioner named Frankie O'Neil, got a verdict from a New York jury that McKetrick's claim for $1,497 would have to come out of the Paris money, which had been frozen by McKetrick himself. Well pleased with this Solomonic decision, O'Neil went to lunch with Moran at Whyte's Restaurant, where they found McKetrick sitting at a table with a fight manager named Harry Pollak and a middleweight known as Young Ahearn.

"How about that, McKetrick?" asked O'Neil as he

passed the promoter's table. McKetrick rose and punched O'Neil in the belly, whereupon O'Neil knocked him over the table in a welter of crockery, clam chowder, and India Pale Ale. McKetrick rolled away before the counselor could put the boots to him, while Pollak jumped up and started wildly throwing punches. The spectacle of managers and a lawyer fighting for nothing was highly satisfactory to Moran and Ahearn, who sat back and drank in the sight. Waiters and customers milled about, the proprietor rushed out screaming, and in the confusion O'Neil made his escape unharmed.

If Johnson had known this retribution would some day overtake McKetrick, it would have given him pleasure but little practical benefit at the end of June, 1914, in Paris. As he recovered from the victory celebration, Jack took inventory: he had lost the $14,400 promised for risking his title against Moran, he owed tremendous bills, his credit had evaporated, and war was threatening. So there was nothing for it but fill all the variety bookings he could get while it was still possible to travel in Europe. Accordingly, he accepted an offer to perform in St. Petersburg, and the three musketeers set out for Russia early in July.

They found St. Petersburg in terrible confusion with mobilizing troops and hysterical officials running around in a frenzy. Johnson's visit was promoted by the same George Thomas who had invited him to Russia the year before, and he was a remarkable man. An American Negro, formerly a valet, Thomas was now Russia's leading producer of sporting events. He also controlled a large amusement park, and billed Johnson as the headline attraction in its outdoor variety theater. Thomas was so well established that he had connections at the court of Czar Nicholas II and attended social functions at the palace. Johnson never ceased to marvel over an introduction his sponsor provided late one night at a gathering of important people. Here Thomas introduced Jack to a strange person, a sort of priest, who was very drunk and none too clean, with a beard, and glittering eyes—Rasputin.

"Some day, somebody gonna *kill* that man," whispered Thomas. But it was Johnson who was nearly annihilated on this occasion, when he tried to stand against the weird monk, drink for drink, at the vodka tables. Johnson got back to his hotel at daylight. A few hours later the police rushed in, made Johnson get dressed and hustled him— suffering with a frightful headache—to the station house. There an official told Johnson to get himself and his party out of Russia. "They invoked the five-and-ten law," Johnson said. "That means five minutes to pack, and ten minutes to get out of town." Through Thomas' influence, Jack and his companions managed to load their fourteen trunks on an outgoing train. Jack later recorded that just as they were leaving Thomas drew him aside, and slipped him a package of papers. Thomas said that these were copies of personal exchanges between the Czar and the German Kaiser. Johnson was to take the documents to London, where Thomas would let him know how to dispose of them. Whatever he entrusted to Johnson, George Thomas played in bad luck from that time on. Enraged at his prosperity, his nationality, and his color, a lynching mob of Bolsheviks drove him out of St. Petersburg (renamed Leningrad) in October, 1917. He settled in Constantinople, but never again was as rich and famous as he had been in the days of the Czar.

Jack's outbound trip was uncomfortable, if not actually perilous, and he recorded that the Russian troops on the train disgusted him with their disorder and filth. At Warsaw, the three musketeers saw the van carrying their trunks roll down a siding and out of their lives forever, but somehow Johnson and his two companions managed to get into another train that put them into Berlin 48 hours later. Here Johnson was told there would be an indefinite wait for a Paris connection. He went for a stroll outside the station, and saw a crowd of Germans preparing to beat a Frenchman to death. Johnson protested, and in the argument committed the awful offense of striking a German civil servant. The Frenchman escaped; police marched Johnson back into the railroad station, where a high official decreed he must leave Germany at once. Above all things this was what Johnson himself wished to do; while he was outside, Gus Rhodes had been distributing bribes, and in a short time the frock-coated station master superintended a squad of porters in giving the mighty push that wedged Lucille, Jack, and Gus aboard a hideously crowded train bound for the Belgian frontier.

The train stopped short of the border, and all passengers were ordered to get out and walk. Beside the track stood a rank of sentries, one of whom recognized the champion. "Run fast, Jack Johnson," said the soldier. "The President of France is assassinated and we will be in Paris in three days." Carrying two suitcases, Jack walked three miles into Belgium. Next day, when Jack and his party at last reached Paris, they found the confusion even greater than at St. Petersburg. Johnson decided to head for London; he went out to Asnières, got his car out of storage, and started for Boulogne. On the way he went off the road at high speed down a 50-foot embankment, but nobody was hurt. With this kind of driving Johnson managed to reach the port over roads that were choked with military traffic, only to arrive in the middle of a stampede of 4,000 calvary horses on the pier. Even more memorable was the sight of British troops disembarking: there were London regiments, and Scots; their marching song had a haunting lilt and was about a place in Ireland. "It's a long way to Tipperary," they were singing, "it's a long way to go. . . ."

Next day in London Johnson visited Tozer and heard that it might now be feasible to arrange substantial bookings throughout the United Kingdom. Tozer believed the public might accept Jack as a means of taking minds off the fears and worries of the war. To test the possibility of such a change of heart about Johnson, the managers took him that night to a large London music hall, where he was to enter a box and be called to the stage for introduction. As he waited, Johnson again heard "Tipperary"—it was the closing number of the turn preceding his appearance. "Come on now—everybody!" cried the performer, and the audience burst into the chorus. Johnson could not resist it. Arms aloft and golden smile agleam, he marched across the front of the house, mounted the stage, and joined the singing. For once he had done the right thing before an English audience.

"Good old Jack!" the audience shouted.

"Good old England!" cried Johnson.

A brief period of cordial relations between Johnson and the British public now began. There had been no change in Jack, but for a few weeks a wave of emotion that can only be called happiness lifted the English people. Rupert Brooke tried to describe this emotion by saying that he could see every aspect of England more sharply than ever before, distinct and clear to the minutest detail, yet bathed in a golden glow. There was a sense of purpose and dedication, coupled with relief that "it had come at last." Johnson made the mistake of thinking this mood of serene public joy, in which any entertainer could flourish, would last indefinitely. He prepared a sketch called *Seconds Out* in which Lucille performed an "Oyster Shell Dance," while he furnished a bass viol accompaniment. Knowingly or not, he was once again exploiting the theme of beauty and the beast. Offstage, Johnson also tried to make a spectacular impression, and at least added the decorative note of fine clothes to the London scene. It is true that the streets were filled with men wearing superb uniforms, and even the elderly men of the middle and upper classes wore excellent shoes, suits, and hats—the world's best. But Johnson's dress during this period was like theatrical costuming; for example, he walked one afternoon down Piccadilly wearing a biscuit-colored silk suit and a pale golden soft hat of the style known as the Trilby, after George du Maurier's heroine. A silk bandana trailed from his jacket pocket, and he tapped the pavement with a black silver-headed walking stick, almost prancing in shoes made of doeskin and crocodile leather. When not walking, Johnson took the air in a white Benz touring car, its top folded back to display leopard-skin upholstery. For a short time, Londoners and the people of the provinces retained their "Good old Jack" mood; but as the casualty lists began to come in, the warmth rapidly went out of Johnson's relations with the British. He was not the type to help people forget those terrible lists. But it can be demonstrated that Johnson's color had nothing to do with the public revulsion. Let us remember that Jim Corbett had appeared with some success as an actor and vaudeville entertainer, and ask ourselves if he could have met the emotional needs of English people at this time. Obviously not; the British needed someone now like Harry Lauder, who could touch their hearts.

The brief era of good feeling, over almost as soon as it began, left Johnson facing a bleak world with few prospects. Money had come in, money had gone out. Troubles piled up: there was a dispute over commissions to vaudeville managers; there was even a summons to the London police court on a charge of using obscene language in public. The charges collapsed, but this was more evidence, though none was needed, that Johnson's remaining days in England would not be happy ones. On the Continent, war; in England, steady dislike; back home in America, jail; these were the alternatives now before Jack Johnson. He showed courage by continuing to smile in public, and by issuing statements that he was going to produce a grand musical revue, and organize a traveling troupe of boxers. There was no interest. Then one morning a message came: Jack Curley was in London and wanted to see Johnson immediately at the Savoy Hotel. Though he complained that he was rising in the middle of the night, Jack got there in time for lunch.

Curley had important news: he had lined up the backers to promote a world heavyweight championship fight.

Johnson's opponent would be the most impressive of the
white hopes, Jess Willard. Jack affected to have forgotten
who this was, and used the French accent he had acquired
since last seeing Curley to drawl, "Who is Weelard?"
Then he put a cigarette into a long tortoise-shell holder.
"Don't give me that stuff," Curley said. He went on to
remark that in case Jack didn't remember, Willard stood
six feet six inches tall, weighed 250 pounds, and was now
sufficiently known to draw a crowd as challenger.

"All right," Johnson said, "I will take this Weelard for
you. Let me know what round."

Curley replied that he was not so much concerned with
what round ended the fight as with finding a place to
hold it. Johnson facing a white hope who had a chance
of beating him would be a tremendous draw anywhere in
the United States, but that could not be, since the champion could hardly defend his title in jail. By Johnson's
account of the meeting, Curley offered some suggestions
in this matter of the jail sentence. In these supposed
recollections, Johnson claimed that Curley told him the
outcome of the fight would determine his treatment when
he returned to the United States.

The discussion was adjourned, to be resumed at dinner.
It was late in the evening, according to Johnson, and over
the brandy and cigars that Curley revealed he had politicians working on the Mann Act trouble, and "the fix
was in." But there was a condition attached to the obtaining of Johnson's liberty: he must lose to Willard. And so,
Johnson wrote in his memoirs, they "reached an agreement, as far as I was concerned, which would give Willard
the championship and permit me to return home."

VI
The Wanderer

With another world championship match in prospect, Johnson was happier than he had been since the money for the Moran fight disappeared. He knew he would be paid this time, as Curley always kept his temper under control and was no man to let lawyers or bankers of any nationality get their hands on box office cash. Curley guaranteed Johnson's share of the money, and that was all he had promised: Jack's tale of being advised to throw the fight to Willard was fantasy. This we shall demonstrate by evidence based on the fight itself; we note it at this point in the narrative to sparc readers the trouble of looking between the lines.

It is true that Johnson did not train for the Willard fight as conscientiously as he prepared for Jim Jeffries. Jack convinced himself that Willard was only a taller Frank Moran; having reached agreement with Curley, he started on a series of parties that appeared to be celebrations of victory in advance; and the champagne sizzled on the ice and brandy in the Rajah's pegs. This led to Bow Street Police Court, where Johnson was brought on a charge of causing a crowd to collect and obstructing traffic. The proceedings were reminiscent of the burlesque show routine called "Irish Justice," which ends with the judge hitting the prisoner on the head with his gavel. Johnson said he could not keep people from looking at him. The beak yelled, "That is no reason why you should go swaggering in Cranbourne Street with your motor-car following you in order to draw attention and create a crowd! I fine you forty shillings!"

So once again Johnson had a demonstration that they did not care for him in England, the country to which he kept returning as though influenced by a dream that some day he and these easy-going people would come to an understanding. At the moment, with the news of the championship match in all the papers, Johnson got an offer to tour the Latin American variety theaters. Jack was glad to go: he played Rio de Janeiro, Buenos Aires, and smaller places with his usual act—Lucille's dance, and some added strong man stunts that could be loosely classified as training. In this part of the program, Johnson lifted weights, broke chains by tensing his muscles, carried four men, pulled a team of horses, and allowed a horse to stand on his chest.

Meanwhile Curley talked to his backers in New York, and announced that the fight would take place in Juarez, Mexico. This place was ruled by the bandit and revolutionist Francisco Villa, but Curley fearlessly traveled to his lair to get permission for the fight. Villa specified that his personal cut of the money should come from the top, but otherwise made no trouble.* There remained the problem

---

* As Mexican politicians go, Villa showed no unusual rapacity; but Curley did not join the mourners when he was killed by government *pistoleros* in 1923.

of getting Johnson to the scene of the match. He would have to pass through a seaport and the central part of the country, where President Venustiano Carranza was in charge. At this point Curley got into difficulties; it appeared that *El Presidente* demanded a larger cut of the boodle than Curley felt he could spare. Negotiations for safe conduct broke down, and Carranza declared to Jack Clancy of the Mexican Pinkerton Bureau that he would seize Johnson if he entered Mexico, and turn him over to the gringo police. Meanwhile, Johnson had worked his way up to Cuba with the musical and strong man act, and Curley decided Havana might be a good place to hold the fight.

Johnson and Curley set final plans when the promoter arrived in Havana to pay the newspapermen and make arrangements with President Mario Menocal. When Curley interviewed the President, he expressed his respectful admiration with a suitable gift, and was told that the match was welcome in Havana. But Cuba was a proud nation. "There must be no scandal," said the statesman as he pocketed his tip. Curley assured him the fight would be sincere and honorable, and withdrew.

With one exception, the Havana journalists felt that their gratuities were adequate, and gave Curley good value in stories about the coming fight. The one disgruntled editor started a campaign to embarrass Curley on the ground that he had scheduled the match for Easter Sunday. Instead of paying the man more money, Curley postponed the fight one day, and thanked him for pointing out an error in judgment. Once more there was talk of "the Battle of the Century," and once more the experts man-

aged to misread the signs as to the probable outcome of
the fight, although in considering the matter today we
must remember that it is easy to be wise after the fact.

However, Jack's public training activities in Cuba were
singularly like those of Jeffries before Reno: he was dis-
inclined to hard work, and slow in his reactions. Willard,
on the other hand, came to Cuba in superb shape, and
went through his exercises and sparring matches with
snap and precision. He was managed by Tom Jones, a
sporting barber from Kewanee, Illinois, who had pawned
his diamond rings to raise betting money. It should not
be supposed that the businesslike air surrounding the
Willard camp daunted Johnson; he expected to knock
Willard out, and went so far as to telegraph friends in
Chicago: "WILL WIN FIFTEENTH ROUND." Since
there could be no conceivable advantage to Johnson in
betraying his friends, some people regarded the telegram
as the equivalent of a sight draft on the First National
Bank. But a Chicago bookie named Jim O'Leary had
doubts as to Johnson's present capability. "I'm afraid of
this thing," the gambler said. "It's too far away, and I don't
know what's going on." He thought of Johnson's thirty-
seven years, and his great feats of eating and drinking,
and reduced the odds against Willard.

Things were heating up in Havana. The disgruntled
editor got to the United States consul and persuaded him
to send a protest against the fight to Washington; this
dispatch was laid before William Jennings Bryan as Secretary of State. The editor and the consul had forgotten, or
did not know, that Curley had once managed a lecture
tour for Bryan and might be on good terms with his former

client. Such was the case: "I know this Jack Curley," said
Bryan, "and he's all right. Besides, I saw a prize fight once,
and it was very interesting." Even if he had disapproved
of Curley's Havana promotion, Bryan would hardly have
called out the Marines; as it was, his endorsement gave
an unexpected lift to the last few days' publicity, and
amounted to a guarantee that Curley would not lose his
investment in the wooden arena that had arisen at the
Oriental Park Racetrack. Here nearly sixteen thousand
people took their places under a blistering sun to watch
the fight on April 5, 1915. About one thousand of the
spectators were women, the largest number yet to watch a
professional boxing match; and among these women, sitting near the ring, was Lucille Johnson.

Willard marched to the ring wearing a ten-gallon
sombrero, and when he took off his robe revealed a flat
stomach that he had hardened through six months of
training. Johnson's middle was flabby, and he looked
small in comparison with Willard as Burns had looked
beside Jack seven years before. Nevertheless, Johnson
started out in an aggressive manner, as a champion should,
and landed some hard blows. "I devoutly hope I didn't
happen to hurt you, Jess," Johnson said after coming out
ahead in an exchange of punches. Here it was again, the
detestable taunting, and the crowd bellowed with rage.
As the fight went on, most of the spectators were pleased
to see that the intense heat appeared to be causing Jack
more distress than Willard. By the eighth round, Johnson
was gasping and panting. When they came out for the
thirteenth round, Johnson got himself together and pummeled Willard smartly, but did not do enough damage to

put him down. This was the high point of the fight so far as Johnson's attack was concerned. Nine rounds later he was hanging on doggedly as the crowd yelled for Willard to finish him off. Sprawled on a stool after the twenty-fourth round, Jack called Curley and an aide named Tom Flanagan to his side, and asked them to escort Lucille from the arena. The champion gasped, "It don't look—too good—right now." Johnson got through the next round, during which Flanagan worked his way to Lucille and took her out; when Jack dragged himself upright for the twenty-sixth round, the crowd sensed the kill. Willard could see that the champion's tired arms had failed him; there was no longer even the semblance of a defense; he moved in confidently and knocked Johnson out with a punch on the chin.

One of the best known of all sporting photographs, for many years a standard wall decoration in saloons and speakeasies, shows Johnson on his back with Willard towering over him. Much has been made of the position of Jack's arms, which seem to be raised as if to shield his eyes from the sun. Generations of barflies have assured one another that this means Johnson knew what he was doing —that he had thrown the fight to Willard. In fact, the picture shows only that Johnson may not have been completely unconscious, any more than Jeffries was at Reno. Like Jeffries, he was finished so far as the fight was concerned.

Also like Jeffries, Johnson spoke frankly about the fight and his part in it shortly after leaving the ring. "Willard was too much for me," he told a reporter. "I just didn't have it."

Johnson soon forgot this moment of truth, and to the fantasy about a promise that his jail term would be remitted if he allowed Willard to win, he added a story that he was to receive $50,000 for throwing the fight. There was much indignation at Johnson for concocting this story, and for sticking to it all his life, as he did. Perhaps now we feel a certain pity for Johnson in this matter, showing as it does his pride in the championship, a feeling so intense that he would rather have it thought he had sold the title than that he lost it to a younger and stronger man. It is not to Johnson's credit that he told this tale, but it would be even more to his discredit if it were true; oddly enough, it is in justice to Johnson's memory that we must proceed to prove that he concocted a lie.

The gist of Johnson's story of the bribe was that Lucille's only purpose in attending the fight was to receive a package of bills from the box office amounting to $50,000. When this transaction was completed, she was to signal her husband in the ring, and then leave the arena, taking the money in her handbag. In his memoirs, Johnson wrote that "the fight was originally intended to end in the 10th round, but when that round arrived, the money had not been paid. It was nearing the 26th round when the money was turned over to Mrs. Johnson. I had specified that it should be in $500 bills so that the package should be small and the amount quickly counted. After examining it she gave me the signal. I replied that everything was O.K. and she departed. In the 26th round I let the fight end as it did. I felt all the way through that I was mastering Willard. I could have disposed of him long before the final round. I was happy because I hopefully looked forward to my speedy return to the United States, where I would again be with my old friends, and above all, with my mother."

Lucille left the arena before the twenty-sixth round, but not to carry a package of $500 bills fresh from the box office. There was no such package; it was an impossibility, and this detail about the face amount of the bills is what completely discredits Johnson's story. How often are bills of that denomination presented at box office windows? Very seldom, yet Johnson would have us believe that at least one hundred $500 bills landed in Curley's till on the day of the fight, and this in the face of the fact that all expensive seats and most of the general admission tickets had been sold in advance. Jack Curley had sympathy for Johnson, but it took him only a few words to dispose of the faked-fight story: "Jack was well past his prime, fat and dissipated, and was worn down and knocked out by a strong, game, and well-conditioned opponent." And Jess Willard said, "If Johnson throwed that fight, I wish he throwed it sooner. It was hotter than hell down there."

Any disinterested student of Johnson's personality would by now have recognized the fantasy life which he lived along with his real one, though that was extraordinary enough for most men. He had fantasied the $500 bills and the promises of immunity back home; in the reality of defeat, he began to wonder if there might not really be something in the idea that he could get a remission of his jail term now that Willard had the championship.

Obsessed with this notion, Johnson wrote to his Chicago lawyers, and the reply was crushing. They assured him that he would go to prison if he returned to the United

States. Jack now had no trouble in persuading himself that someone had let him down; and for the next seven years he was so embittered by the thought that he was hard to handle, and occasionally dangerous. The immediate problem was money; Curley had given him the British distribution rights for the moving pictures of the Havana fight, and Johnson returned to London in the hopes of making a fortune with the films.

Almost at once, Johnson's sense of injustice was aggravated by the trouble he had in getting delivery of the prints. Terribly tangled in wartime red tape, Johnson had finally got his hands on the reels at the express office in London when suddenly a Mr. A. Weil appeared and tried to take them away from him. It was impossible to find out who this A. Weil was representing; he was so sure of the justice of his cause, whatever it was, that he seized several cans of film and started to run away with them. Johnson roared with anger, leaped on A. Weil, and bent him badly out of shape. Though it seems beyond belief, there was no charge of assault, and Jack was allowed to keep his property. For the time being, this put him back in his "Good old England" mood.

That was too good to last, of course, and Johnson was soon in ugly trouble. He had put on an enlarged version of *Seconds Out* before tepid audiences at the Hippodrome in Preston, and got into a dispute with the company manager, Jack du Maurier, who was a minor show business functionary, not to be confused with Sir Gerald du Maurier, old Harrovian and West End star. The disagreement with Jack du Maurier became so acrimonious that the man resigned and asked for his fare back to London, in addition

to other sums due him. At this final interview Johnson lost
his temper and struck du Maurier, injuring his left eye to
such an extent that he later received a court judgment
of £1,075 in damages. Johnson did not confine his bad
temper to theatrical colleagues; he began to lash out at
all and sundry, and caused a distressing scene in a pub
by uttering pro-German sentiments when drunk. The
British were deep in the war, with agonizing casualty lists
growing day by day; in France, the infantry called the
deadly German 5.9 inch cannon the "Jack Johnson." One
can imagine the disgust of the British at the conduct of
the real Jack Johnson on their home front. He himself
realized now that when he met with dislike, it was not
altogether because of envy at his automobile and fine
clothes. Yet like many sensitive people, Johnson could be
unfeeling where others were concerned. It was astounding
to him when he and Lucille came back from the theater
one evening to find that their apartment had been entered
and their belongings turned out on the floor. The only
thing missing was the packet of papers Johnson had
brought from Russia at the request of George Thomas.
Incredible as Johnson's tale of these secret papers may be,
the rifling of his apartment is a matter of record. It is also
a fact that a few evenings later a man stepped up to Johnson on the street and said, "You are Mr. Jack Johnson?"
When Jack nodded, the man placed a paper in his hand.
Johnson did not drop the document as he would have done
had he been facing a mere process server. This was a person with a military mustache, a tan raincoat, a bowler hat,
and a grim official air that spelled police. A voice came
from under the mustache, the lips scarcely moving: "It

is my duty to give you this order to leave England within twenty-four hours."

The expulsion order had originated in the Home Office, under a piece of emergency legislation similar to that which had caused a readjustment in the hours for the sale of drink in public houses, along with many other regulations of greater and less import. Students of Johnson's career believe his pro-German remarks brought matters to a head. His ousting from Russia also was held against him in making the case that he was an undesirable alien and a handicap to the war effort. Officials in government offices had been annoyed with Johnson for some time; indeed from the days of his first visit to England there had been complaints of noise, bad language, and difficulties in getting him to settle his bills. Now there was the attack on du Maurier, and, more recently, a claim by lithographers that they had not been paid for posters advertising *Seconds Out*. Johnson's defense was that he had not ordered the posters, that their wording was wrong, and that what they presented as his picture bore no resemblance to him. All this may have been true, but the jury found for the plaintiffs; in making their decision, these ordinary Englishmen reflected the dislike for Johnson that was agitating powerful dignitaries far above them in the structure of British authority.

Johnson sensed the weight of disapproval behind the expulsion order accurately enough, but could not bring himself to accept it as final. The paper had been handed to him in the first week of January, 1916; instead of packing up at once he decided to appeal to an influential fellow American, and the following morning found him calling on Sir Hiram Maxim, inventor of the Maxim machine gun and now a naturalized British citizen living at Streatham. The white-bearded sage received Johnson without enthusiasm. All he could produce in the way of advice was that Jack might speak to Lord Lonsdale, for the first sportsman of England was presumably the patron of all athletes, including professional boxers.

A short time afterward, Johnson was in Carlton House Terrace waiting for an interview with Lonsdale. This remarkable old man was known as "the Yellow Earl" because of his extreme partiality to that color, and when Johnson was ushered into the morning room, he observed that the hangings, upholstery, and wallpaper were all in Lonsdale's favorite tint. The Earl was seated in an armchair, stroking the lean head of a borzoi, and he greeted Johnson cordially. (Fortunately for Jack, Lonsdale was a more kindly and helpful sort of man than his ancestor, the first Earl, who smashed windows, baited constables, and stole James Boswell's wig.)

"I will do what I can, Johnson," said Lonsdale, when he heard his visitor's story. "Sportsmen must always stick together, you know. But we live in strange times. . . . Now tell me about your fight with Jim Jeffries."

After chatting for a while, Lonsdale ended the interview by rising and walking with his guest into the outer hall. "You can rely on me to do my best," he said. A footman came with Jack's overcoat. "Let me help you, Johnson," said the peer, taking the coat and holding it out. Till the day he died, Johnson kept the memory of this small courtesy bright; there were not many men who could say the greatest gentleman in England had helped them into a coat.

Jack's next stop was at the office of his solicitor, who gave an opinion that he might enter an appeal against the ouster, and possibly win it, and that in any event he could remain in England until the appeal came up in court. Johnson drew from this the erroneous conclusion that his troubles were over. In the euphoria of the Lonsdale visit, he held several noisy parties, and made himself more noticeable than ever in London and the surrounding countryside. In order to explain what happened next, one must examine evidence that seems to indicate the reaching of a decision deep in the recesses of the Home Office. Reduced to plain words, that decision might be stated: "We cannot allow this fellow Johnson to take us into court. Something must be done to make him leave England of his own volition. This is a case in which the end justifies the means."

It may be inferred that this purpose became known somewhere in the apparatus the government maintained for unacknowledgable acts. Someone made plans, and money passed; and a few nights later, the doorman at a West End pub said to Johnson as he was leaving the place, "Do you know you're being followed?" Jack thought the man was either joking or mistaken, but late the following night, as he entered a side street off Shaftesbury Avenue, Johnson heard footsteps on the pavement, and turned to see several thugs closing in. Jack disabled one of them with a street fighter's kick as a hoodlum tried for his eyes with the buckle of a heavy belt, missed, and opened a gash on his cheek, the only scar he ever carried from a fight in or out of the ring. Failing to down Johnson on the first rush, the rowdies drew off to organize another attack. IIe had backed against a shop window, and at that mo-

ment he would have pledged his entire future earnings
for a knife or pistol. These were professionals, and with
the next rush they would get him on the pavement and
blind him, or kill him by jumping on his chest and crushing his heart under the broken ribs. As suddenly as it had
come upon him, this frightful prospect now disappeared as
two policemen turned the corner. When they saw the blue
uniforms and helmets, the thugs crossed the street and
hurried out of sight, helping the injured man along as
though he were a friend who had taken too much whiskey.
The policemen walked toward Johnson and asked him
what the trouble was. "I don't feel too good," Johnson said.
"Would you help me to a cab on Shaftesbury Avenue?"
The bobbies did as he asked.

Next day was the first of March, 1916, and along with its
lists of officers and men killed in France the *Times* announced that Jack Johnson was leaving the country,
"having decided to obey a ruling of the Home Office under
the Aliens Restriction Act." Along with Lucille and Gus
Rhodes, Jack was headed for Spain by way of South
America. And though the three muskcteers carried their
usual heavy consignment of baggage, Jack's pocketbook
was lighter than he liked. He had collected £3,000 by
exhibiting the Havana films, but *Seconds Out* had been a
disappointment. First class travel for three people halfway
around the world from London to Barcelona made the
money vanish like fairy gold that melts at the frontier.
Johnson therefore was on the alert for any kind of business
opening; his first venture in Barcelona was an attempt to
start an advertising agency. The plan was for Jack to act
as contact man while others prepared copy and art work.

This scheme showed imagination and intelligence on Johnson's part, but he failed to interest the professional advertising people he needed to put the agency into operation.

A more practical means of earning money was to perform as star of a moving picture for a Spanish producer. The central figure of a screen drama called *False Nobility*, Johnson took part in staged fights with other actors, with boa constrictors, and with lions. He then turned to wrestling, and got a fair return from several bouts that attracted good crowds. But wrestling had little importance in Spain; Johnson could see that bullfighting was by far the most popular sport in the country. He met the great matadors Joselito and Belmonte, who took a liking to him and suggested he enter their profession. They told Jack he would draw well at the box office, if only as a freak. And he might become good; he could still move fast when he wanted to. Accordingly, they began training Johnson with small bulls.

In return, Johnson offered his friends a course of boxing lessons. The small and frail Belmonte was not interested, but Joselito, a sturdy six-footer, was an enthusiastic pupil. Looking back on this period in his old age, Johnson recalled that Joselito had talent. He added, "But there was one bad fault—he stood too open." Johnson held the opinion that Joselito carried this fault into the bull ring, where it ultimately caused his death.

After intensive coaching by the two stars, Johnson entered the arena as a professional matador for the first time on July 10, 1916, at Barcelona. Jack thought his personal safety was not involved, as he had the impression that the drawing of bulls would be so arranged that he would not be confronted by a ferocious animal in his debut. He became apprehensive, however, when he marched out in the ceremonial opening procession and detected a bloodthirsty tone in the yells of the largest crowd he had ever seen. It dawned on him then that these people were gathered in the pure Latin hope of seeing him impaled or disemboweled by a bull's horn. In addition Jack was suffering acute discomfort from the tightness of the trousers of his splendid traditional costume. He realized he should have taken warning from a dream that had disturbed him the night before: a funeral, with hundreds of mourners, and himself as the central figure. It was too late now. . . .

The gate crashed open. Instead of a small and friendly animal, an enormous bull rushed out, spoiling for a fight. Somebody had lied to Jack about the drawing; this was a bull of the Miura strain, the breed of death. However, he managed to dispatch the creature, though he had to stab it three times. Though they would have preferred to witness his death, the members of the audience were moved by Jack's courage, and gave him the heartiest cheers he had ever heard; and Belmonte shook his hand. It was a good beginning. If Johnson had applied himself to the bullfighter's trade and become fully aware of the Spanish temperament, which was in so many ways like his own, he might have found in Spain a long career and an honored old age. But Jack refused to take bullfighting seriously; that he also no longer took boxing seriously had been shown when he fought the poet Arthur Cravan, on April 29, 1916, at Barcelona.

The most extraordinary of all Johnson's opponents, Cravan had been born Fabian Avernus Lloyd in Lausanne, of English parents, and was twenty-nine when he faced Johnson in the ring. He had gone to the United States at the age of seventeen and worked his way from New York to California as a chauffeur and boxer. According to his biographer Bernard Delvaille, Cravan next turned up in Berlin, where he lived in a world of homosexuals, prostitutes, and thieves. A disciple of Mallarmé, Rimbaud, and Baudelaire, he became known for his poetry as well as for his skill at boxing and swimming in Berlin, Paris, and Munich. In 1914, he spent eight days in jail for beating a woman. When the World War broke out, Cravan went to Barcelona to avoid British military service. His objective was New York, and he took the match with Johnson to raise money for the fare. The fight was unexciting; though powerful, the writer was overmatched with Johnson, who sparred in graceful style for a few rounds to show off his flawless defense, and then knocked Cravan out. Next day, Cravan left for New York City. He became a well known figure in bohemian circles, but earned so little with his writing and boxing that he was sometimes compelled to sleep in Central Park.

Johnson showed that he was not governed by convention when he fought such an odd character as Arthur Cravan; he also showed during this period that he had no objection to unconventional warfare. German submarines were in Spanish waters, and when the United States entered the war on April 6, 1917, it became necessary to start coast-watching operations from La Coruna to Bilbao, and other confidential missions had to be performed in neutral Spain. Johnson got in touch with Major Lang, the U. S. military attaché in Madrid, offering his services for espionage and informal combat. This fitted Johnson's taste for melodrama, and the close security over all such operations made them rich material for fantasy. For this reason one must read Johnson's memoirs of the period with care. There is no question that coast watching and the discouragement of similar activities by German agents could also blend conveniently with business suitable to remote coastal inlets and moonless nights, when various sorts of contraband might be moved. There were members of the American colony in Madrid who mentioned Johnson's name in connection with smuggling. Be that as it may, situations rose in which Johnson was useful. There was, for example, the case of the captain of a Danish tramp steamer who was known to be fueling U-boats and giving them surface navigational aids. The captain was a pugnacious man, and joined his crew in a fight with Americans when his activities were questioned in a waterfront tavern. Shortly afterward, the Dane ran into something or somebody that put him out of commission—almost killed him, in fact. He was not heard from again, and Johnson got credit for the near-kill, which took place when anonymous persons boarded the tramp in a deserted cove.

Johnson also tried to get financial credit on the strength of his clandestine operations, and in this connection a State Department document has come to light. On April 13, 1918, the American consul at Malaga wrote to Ambassador Joseph E. Willard at Madrid as follows: "I have the honor to report that Jack Johnson, ex-champion pugilistic (sic) of the United States, called at this consu-

13. Jack Johnson and Deputy Sheriff Billy Silver at the U.S. border, July 20, 1920. Silver delivered Johnson to federal authorities.

14. Johnson with his fourth and last wife, Irene, returning from Europe on the S.S. Bremen, 1932.

15. Ettore Nava, baritone, as Amonasro, Alfredo Salmaggi, director of the Hippodrome Opera Company, and Jack Johnson as an Ethiopian general—*Aida*, 1936.

16. Jack Johnson was 53 years old when he faced Dynamite Jackson in a three-round bout at Los Angeles. Johnson won.

late today and requested me to notify the Hotel Regina
where he is staying that he would meet his bill for board.
In this connection, he informed me confidentially that he
was employed by Major Lang and that he expected money
from him. Jack Johnson was informed that this consulate
was unwilling to make guarantees for anyone. The above
is brought to the attention of the Embassy for its information. I have the honor to be, sir, Your obedient servant,
Louis G. Dreyfus, Jr., American Consul."

Connoisseurs of State Department language may relish
that dispatch for its style at the same time that they
wonder if Dreyfus was wise in risking Johnson's cover by
writing it. It is known that Johnson left the consulate with
dignity, but what he did next is shrouded in the fog of war,
and the shadows that surround all intelligence procedures.
Whatever happened, it inspired another fine piece of State
Department prose, dated almost a year later, four months
after the end of the war. Writing from London to a Washington official named L. Lanier Winslow, a State Department bureaucrat named Edward Bell had this to report:
"I want to give you a little information about your colored
friend, Mr. John Arthur Johnson, otherwise known as Jack
Johnson, the former heavyweight champion. From an
Instruction No. 165 of June 4, 1915, from the Department,
in which Jack is described as a colored person of wide
reputation in the pugilistic world, I gather that he is a
fugitive from the justice of the United States, and is not
likely to set foot in his native land in the immediate future.
It may interest you to know that in the course of the past
year, while he was in Spain, he offered his services to the
German organization in that country for the purposes of

espionage against the Allies, including his native country. The German organization in Spain referred his application to Berlin, where it was turned down. So far as I know, Jack never engaged in espionage against us. It was not his fault, however, and I think it just as well that this should be borne in mind." It also should be borne in mind, as we read the files today, that Johnson may have been acting on instructions in treating with the Germans, and attempting the hazardous role of double agent. It is significant that no action was ever taken against Johnson for approaching the enemy. And no known citation was issued for service to the American side.

Johnson left Spain in April of 1919 and went to Mexico City. Taking Lucille and Gus Rhodes with him, he made the move at the invitation of a group of sportsmen who suggested that he promote boxing and wrestling, and engage in bullfighting on the side. He seemed to have entered a likely field, for with the end of the war Mexico City had become a tourist center, full of Americans on holiday. The city had also become headquarters for a swarm of international drunks, spies, broken-down newspapermen, fences for stolen jewelry and paintings, and propagandists for all brands of politics. Johnson found it all to his taste, and took the lead in a hard-drinking circle of military men and *Cientificos,* or mining millionaires, who lived in baroque mansions and breakfasted every day promptly at seven P.M.

The railway magnate Paulino Fontes was a member of this set and he took Johnson out to call on President Carranza in the palace at Chapultapec. Carranza forgot his difficulties with Jack Curley when he welcomed the boxer and said, "You are a man of experience, Mr. Johnson, and you have met all sorts of people. I would rather listen to you than hear an oration from a professional politician. I can learn more from you." Others who had an opportunity to learn from Johnson were the seedy heavyweights whom he defeated in the ring for the edification of Fontes and the syndicated sportsmen. The victims included Marty Cutler, George De Bray, Jack Heinan, the Englishman Tom Cowler, and Captain Bob Roper, a soldier of fortune.

An old opponent turned up at this time when Arthur Cravan arrived in town. The poet had gone from New York to Canada before coming to Mexico City to lecture on Egyptian art and open a boxing academy, which Johnson kindly recommended to his friends. Less than a year later, Cravan disappeared. Some said he had been stabbed in a nightclub brawl, the crime being overlooked by the police because they thought he was an American. Others maintained that he was knocked on the head and thrown from a boat off Acapulco. As in the case of Ambrose Bierce, the body was never found, and to this day no one knows what happened to the oddity who called himself Arthur Cravan.

Johnson's activities included bullfighting, and he killed a number of the animals to the great joy of Mexicans and *turistas* who flocked to the arena whenever his name appeared in the announcements. It is logical to suppose that Johnson, with his natural grace, gave a good performance in the bull ring. And we should note that because of his size, he made small bulls look puny. He had to take the big ones, and thus he proved for all time that there was no yellow in Jack Johnson.

That Jack was not idle on the intellectual side of Mexican life was shown by his contribution of $20 to the American journalist Carleton Beals for the founding of a literary magazine. This may explain the telegram from A. A. Adee, a State Department official in Washington, to the American Embassy in Mexico, which read: "It has been reported that Jack Johnson, of pugilistic fame, has been spreading social equality propaganda among the Negroes in Mexico and has been endeavouring to incite colored element in this country. Please report any activity of this character on the part of Johnson as well as the manner in which his propaganda is distributed."

As an American citizen, Johnson might have been alarmed at figuring in such a dispatch; but as a friend of President Carranza, he had little to worry about so long as Carranza remained in office. That period was coming to an end: the strong man in Mexico was General Alvaro Obregón, who was approaching Mexico City with an army; and he had sworn to kill Carranza. Making his plans for a fast getaway, Carranza was thoughtful enough to send warning to Johnson that the outgoing President's friends would be dangerously unpopular with Obregón and his followers. It would be pleasant to record that this friend and admirer of Johnson escaped to live on his boodle for years in Paris and Switzerland. But the unhappy fact is that Obregón's people caught up with Carranza before he reached the coast, and shot him. Obregón seized power and lived on the fat of the land until 1928, when the *pistoleros* of a rival faction killed him.

As for Jack, his luck held good during the perilous days of Obregón's accession, and he got out of Mexico City unharmed. His destination was Tia Juana, just below the U. S. line in Lower California, where he planned to open a saloon and promote prize fights. The only way to reach Tia Juana was to proceed overland to Mazatlan and then travel by boat up the Gulf of California. Accompanied by Lucille and Gus, Johnson arranged passage with the captain of a motor yacht. After they set out, Jack found that the skipper had 50 Chinamen below decks who were to be smuggled into the U.S.A. Johnson recorded later that these Orientals were "of a type not particularly inviting as associates." That night a bad storm rose and things looked dubious for a while. The Chinamen went mad with fear and Johnson had to knock a couple of them kicking while the captain, the cook, and the lone deckhand managed the boat. Next morning they steered into the Colorado River, up which they traveled to a lonely bend where the captain dropped anchor to repair the damage of the storm. Johnson, Lucille, and Gus went on land to stretch their legs. During this stroll, Johnson mistakenly thought he saw bandits approaching and fired a pistol, wounding Gus in the arm. They left Gus in a hospital at Mexicali; the Johnsons reached Tia Juana next day.

Less than a year later, after only modest success in promoting fights, Johnson faced what was in his mind: a return to the United States, and to his real home town of Chicago. He would not see his mother: Tina had died in 1917. But he was still comparatively young, and he decided he could not endure spending the rest of his life in exile. With his incorrigible optimism, Jack still could make himself believe that somebody would work

out a settlement of his trouble with the law. He based
this belief partly on a visit from an old friend named Tom
Carey, a wealthy brick manufacturer and politician from
Chicago, now living in Los Angeles, who came down to
visit Jack at Tia Juana. Carey's advice was that Johnson
should come home. He made no promises; he merely said
that whatever happened, it would be best in the long run
for Johnson to return. In this he was right, and Johnson
knew it. And on that clear early summer evening, with
the stars glittering over the desert as they had ten years
before at Reno, Jack said, "All right, Tom—tell them I'm
coming over." A few days later he surrendered to Federal
officers at San Diego.

VII
Last Round

Johnson's surrender took place on July 20, 1920, and brought out headline type of a size the newspapers had not used since the Armistice. Beneath the black letters, there was little to record: Lucille carried a small Mexican hairless dog, Johnson was in good humor; it was said that the Federal men relieved him of a pair of dice. There were no handcuffs. Johnson said, "I've come back to straighten out that mixup with the government, and then look up that fellow, what's his name?—Dempsey?" Asked about the Willard fight, he said, "That was a frame."

Large crowds appeared all across the country wherever Johnson's train passed through a station, and it was observed that the many white persons in these gatherings seemed amiably disposed, in contrast to some who had gathered along his path in other days. There was so much excitement in the Chicago Negro community that the police declared people might be killed in the crush if Johnson appeared in the city. The small Chicago satellite of Geneva was as close as the authorities dared bring him, and there they placed him in the town jail to await judgment.

There was no doubt that the general attitude toward

Johnson had changed. Where it had been condemnatory, the public mood now was kindly and forgiving, and Johnson's captors reflected this amelioration of sentiment by appointing him turnkey of the Geneva jail. This was not merely for the honor of the thing; it was intended to make it possible for Jack to come and go at discretion on business outside the prison walls. In light captivity, Johnson sent as messenger to lawyers in Chicago the faithful Gus Rhodes, who had recovered from his wound. Jack's legal position was not so simple as one might have supposed; from a common sense point of view, here was a fugitive from justice, duly convicted on lawful charges in open court. But there was an odd complication: Johnson's conviction had been *partially* reversed. In April, 1914, while Jack was shuttling between London and Paris, the appeals court had sent back the convictions on the prostitution charges for re-trial if the government could find additional evidence, otherwise to be thrown out; only the convictions on charges of transportation for immoral purposes stood up in the higher court. Thus Johnson was cleared of the only anti-social charges that had lain against him; yet he remained in danger of the penintentiary because of private conduct.

Now that seven years had gone by, Johnson's lawyers pleaded for a lenient judicial view: surely the past conduct of an aging boxer, gambler, and vaudeville trouper stood far down on the nation's list of things to worry about. Indeed, the war had brought a fundamental change of opinion as to the practicality of moral controls. The Mann Act has spoken of immoral purposes—yet such purposes abounded in the United States and elsewhere. And in spite of all efforts by guilt-ridden humanity to live on a higher plane, a large section of Hell reported a vast new paving program. Johnson had never been a public-spirited man, and he lacked the temperament to derive any satisfaction from serving as a moral scapegoat.

Jack was to plead for mercy before George A. Carpenter, who had sentenced him, but legal processes came to a halt because the judge fell ill. In Geneva, Gus brought word that Carpenter might be out of action for a month at least. "Hard lines, eh?" said Jack. "I'm sorry to hear the judge is sick. Yes, indeed. Very sorry."

Nearly three months passed before Carpenter felt able to return to work; Johnson appeared before him on September 14. From the moment the judge began talking, Jack knew he did not have a chance. "I can see no reason for making a change in the sentence," said Carpenter. "If the conduct of the defendant had been such as to indicate that he regretted his criminal act, I might feel differently about a reduction of sentence. On the contrary, Johnson has behaved in a manner to indicate a complete disregard for the laws and institutions of this country." And with that, he ordered Jack to "The Walls"—the Federal penitentiary at Leavenworth, Kansas—to serve out his time of a year and a day.

"I'm sore," Johnson said as the marshals took him out. "They didn't give me a fighting chance. A stiff reprimand would have been sufficient."

However, Johnson's stay at The Walls could have been worse. Upon admission he was brought to the Superintendent, who turned out to be an old friend from the Reno days, ex-Governor Denver S. Dickerson. After losing office in Nevada, this good man had found a snug berth in the government prison service, and he now talked to Johnson in a fatherly way.

"You play square with me, Jack," said Dickerson, "and you won't find things too bad here. Now what job do you want while you're with us?"

Jack put in for prison physical director, and it was so ordered. His duties were to organize and direct the calisthenic drills, and in addition he fought two heavyweights brought from outside to entertain the inmates. Jack had certain privileges: he was allowed to keep a supply of liquor and cigars, and to employ his own cook from among the prisoners. He also had his personal butcher, a trusty who supplied him with 'possum meat. An unpleasantness occurred when Jack invited three friends to supper, and the trusty provided a skinned and butchered cat instead of a 'possum. This fooled the chef, but not Johnson. Unable to deal with the dishonest sutler himself, he arranged for others to give the man a beating.

Johnson was released on July 9, 1921, and as a favor to Superintendent Dickerson delivered an inspirational address to the entire prison population before checking out. At this point, Jack was beginning to feel his way into a vocation as informal exhorter toward the better things of life. In his talk to the prisoners, he took no particular subject; when asked about it, he said he had covered a great deal of ground, "having for my topics religion, squareness, courage, and successful living." The prisoners gave three cheers, and Dickerson escorted Johnson to the gate. Except for violations of speed limits, he was never again in trouble with the law.

While it appeared certain that the general public would now tolerate Johnson, the Chicago police were still nervous about his impact on their city. They remembered the deadly riots that had taken place on the South Side only two years before, and feared that Johnson's appearance might so excite the Negro population that dangerous friction with whites might ensue. Jack announced he would be in Chicago on the morning of July 14, and a strong force of uniformed men and detectives waited for his train to come in. Negro dignitaries were present, but the crowd was nothing like so large as that which had welcomed Johnson after the fight at Reno. When Jack and Lucille got off the train, a member of the reception committee handed them a huge basket of flowers. Through an error in plans, the brass band that was to have serenaded Jack did not appear, and when told of this he said, "Chicago and my friends look mighty good to me with or without the music." Then he said he was ready to fight Jack Dempsey, and invited everyone within the sound of his voice to come along with him for the rest of the day's events. Twelve hours later, Johnson was still a center of attention as hundreds of Negroes pressed around him on South State Street and touched his arms and shoulders when they could not shake his hand. A reception by Negro aldermen and city officials at the Eighth Regiment Armory concluded the day.

The next stop was New York, where two prominent Harlem sporting men named Barron Wilkins and Dick Ellis gave a grand ball in Jack's honor. Johnson then took to the road in vaudeville, attracting much less condemnation—and smaller audiences—than would have been the case a short time before. But the years that now came on, though never prosperous, were by no means quiet and secluded. Johnson continued to develop a gift for extemporaneous chatter, in a mystical, allusive style not unlike that of the Negro cult leader who called himself Father Divine. By the late twenties, Johnson's lectures had taken a moralizing turn, and he appeared in the pulpit on numerous occasions to exhort church audiences. He said that when preaching, he set no text, but wove his discourse around Job, Saul, Esau, Jacob, Esther, and Revelations. He preached to a gathering of Methodist bishops, urging them to keep control of themselves in every situation, and above all to avoid liquor, which could get hold of a man before he knew it and drag him to disaster. Perhaps the most remarkable public speech Johnson ever made was in 1924 at Danville, Illinois. In this appearance he addressed a Klavern of the Ku Klux Klan on sportsmanship, fair play, and the Golden Rule.

That was the year in which Lucille Cameron Johnson ended her marriage to Jack in a New York divorce court; the uncontested charge was infidelity. There was little public moralizing, but here and there a man or woman possessed of sympathy and human curiosity paused to think that Lucille had passed as strange a dozen years as ever fell to the lot of an American girl, including as they did imprisonment, a flight from justice, and a career of notoriety against backgrounds of war and revolution in Europe, England, Mexico, and Spain. To her credit, Lucille Johnson gave no interviews, did not sell her story to the newspapers, and retired to deliberate obscurity.

Early in the summer of 1925, Jack married again. The

bride was Irene Marie Pineau, handsome and blonde like Johnson's other two white wives. A short time before the wedding, she had divorced Harry J. Pineau, an advertising man who liked to spend an afternoon at the racetrack now and then. And it was at the races that Jack met Irene Pineau, the same surroundings in which he first saw Etta Duryea. But Irene Johnson lived a happier life than Etta's had ever been. Quiet and discreet, she avoided publicity and refused to be drawn into controversy of any kind.

Though now in his middle forties, Johnson still fought when he could get a match. For example, he faced a heavyweight named Homer Smith in Montreal on his forty-sixth birthday, gaining the decision in ten rounds. This sort of fight brought in but little money; there was a cruel reduction in Jack's earning power. Under this pressure, he tried a number of vocations, and somehow managed always to have a roof over his head, good clothes on his back, and a fast car to drive. The matter of speed had a significance that Jack failed to recognize, though he appeared in traffic courts with ominous regularity. He went off the road in Connecticut in 1924, and escaped alive from a bad wreck outside Benton Harbor in Michigan the following year. "I must confess to having a weakness for fast driving," Johnson said, and later announced that he intended to enter professional racing. Fortunately he received so little encouragement that he abandoned this idea.

If Jack Johnson failed to make a fortune in his latter years it was not for lack of trying. He tried to promote fights, to represent a Canadian brewery, to sell stocks and bonds, and to produce *Othello* with himself in the title role. He appeared briefly as master of ceremonies and nominal owner of a Los Angeles nightclub—the project foundering in suits and summonses over wages and bills. During the stay at Los Angeles, Jack accepted a few days' work at the Warner Brothers lot, hoping for a break in pictures. At this time a remarkable man named Wilson Mizner was working for the Warners as a dialogue writer. A successful Broadway playwright, Mizner was also by his own admission a swindler and thief, and he had a wide acquaintance among sporting people, including Jack Johnson. So it was that when he heard his old friend was on the premises, Mizner left the throne-like chair in which he slept most of the day, and hurried out to embrace Johnson, and tell the studio officials that here was no bit-player, but a person of importance and distinction. As a result, everyone was polite; but no serious work was offered. In the closing years of his life, the steadiest employment Johnson had was lecturing in Hubert's Museum, the noted collection of educated fleas, fortune-telling machines, circus freaks, and sideshows which is still in business on West Forty-second Street in New York City.

Johnson appeared in "sparring contests" and "exhibition bouts" until 1945, when he was in his sixty-eighth year. The line between a boxing exhibition and a match with a winner and loser not always being clear, the records cannot be trusted as to exactly when Jack fought his last serious fight. One of the last, without question, was in 1926 when he beat Pat Lester in the bull ring at Nogales in fifteen rounds. Lester was a strong young heavyweight who had never been defeated and was thought to be a contender for the championship then held by Jack Demp-

sey. The wire services reported the forty-eight year old
Johnson in great form, picking off punches as a shortstop
catches a ball, and joking with friends from the Twenty-
Fifth Infantry, whose camp was just across the border.

Toward the close of the 1920s, a distinction he had long
wished for came at last to Johnson. This was the recognition that he stood among the few superlative practitioners
of his craft. The official publication on boxing was the
magazine *The Ring*, and in 1927 it stated that "Jack Johnson is the greatest heavyweight of all time." The editor
and publisher of *The Ring* was Nat Fleischer, generally regarded as the sport's most authoritative historian; fifteen
years later, Fleischer summed up his judgment by writing
in his book *The Heavyweight Championship* that Johnson
achieved the highest rating of all boxers in all-around
ability—feinting, hitting, blocking, and counterpunching.
"After years devoted to the study of heavyweight fighters,"
said Fleischer, "I have no hesitation in naming Jack Johnson as the greatest of them all."

This was like the recognition that comes to a fine actor
in retirement from critics who know and love the theater,
and Jack relished and cherished every word. What made
the close of his life unhappy and unsatisfactory was the
withholding of an equally cordial recognition of his worth
as a person. Somehow there was lingering resentment and
disapproval; it was often reflected on the sports pages,
where reporters who were nowhere as competent in writing as Johnson had been in boxing never passed up an
opportunity to refer to him with a sneer. We may take as
an example the treatment he received in *The New York
Times*. The reporter was Arthur Daley, who wrote in

various connections that Johnson was "not a decent character with the nobility of a Louis," and that he was "a man
without principle," and "a wrong guy."

Both white and black politicians sensed the disapproba-
tion attached to Johnson and did their best to keep out
of his way. On occasion, Jack would catch them in public,
as he did to the amusement of Westbrook Pegler by
stopping beside Jim Farley's aisle seat after being introduced from the ring at one of Jack Sharkey's fights in 1929.
Pegler wrote: "In this diplomatic crisis, a strange expression overspread Mr. Farley's features. It was a far-away
expression, such as cartoonists generally ascribe to a gentleman who has stooped to pick up a lady's glove and
heard his trousers rip." But Farley accepted Johnson's
outstretched hand.

Jack seldom had a chance to speak to so great a man
as Jim Farley; he dealt now mostly with the lesser kind of
carnival promoter, and with bill-collectors, litigious lawyers, and the magistrates of small-claims courts, who were
frequently called on to decide on matters of contract and
indebtedness involving Johnson. One such dispute concerned a promoter named Morris Botwen, who asked for
$360.96 to satisfy claims in a deal for the manufacture
and sale of a preparation called Old Champ Liniment.
Johnson explained to the court, "I figured out the formula
years ago. I have given it away to friends for years, and
they all say it will cure toothaches, headaches, or any
other kind of ache. I just refused to make personal appearances for Botwen because I didn't think the stuff he was
making was the same as my product."

Such disagreements would arise because Johnson's main

source of income was appearing as a sideshow attraction at Hubert's in the winter time, and at Coney Island or in small circuses during the summer. His act was mostly what it had been in days of the Hammerstein time and *Seconds Out*—a medley of bag-punching, muscle-flexing, and talk; but he no longer sang or danced. Jack would size up the crowd and tailor the entertainment to its mood. Sometimes he would ask people in his audience what he should talk about; they usually asked for his account of the Reno fight, or his opinion of Jack Dempsey or Joe Louis. Yet even in this innocuous performance, Johnson sometimes managed to give offense; what it came down to was a suspected impudence "in the way he looked at the white women in the audience," as a New York advertising man put it. People would ask each other, "Wasn't there something *about* him? Wasn't he in jail for kidnapping a white girl?" In some mysterious way, it would seem that Johnson had an attraction similar to that of the frightening gorilla named Gargantua, who was exhibited for years in the Ringling Brothers and Barnum & Bailey Circus, surrounded by armed guards.

But in these closing years Johnson was no menace; a sideshow performer and peddler of nostrums could not afford trouble with anyone, and Johnson's awareness of his position grew as his strength decreased. Indeed, his manner became more and more ingratiating as time went by. Even his appearance altered: he began to look like an old-fashioned Southern butler, except that he wore smart double-breasted coats, set off by a beret, spats, and the traditional showman's cane.

At the Chicago World's Fair in 1934 Johnson presided

at a booth, ringing the changes on his time-tried routine before crowds that were sometimes depressingly small. George Lytton had died, but there was another Chicagoan who observed Johnson with interest, in the person of Gilmer Black, a gifted architect and a sportsman. Black was aware of the pathos in Johnson's performance, but did not detect any sentimentality in Jack's conduct or general approach to life. "He was extremely affable," the perceptive architect recorded, "and most remarkably light on his feet." Black was entertained to see Johnson join Samuel Insull and Sally Rand autographing a drum, and appear in an exhibition bout with the veteran heavyweight Sailor Tom Sharkey. For this match, in Referee Dave Barry's "Garden of Champions," Johnson wore conventional ring dress, while Sharkey was costumed in green tights with a sash of red, white, and blue around his middle. Sharkey rushed at his opponent, but Johnson easily held him off or pinioned his arms, flashing the old smile at the spectators and reproving Sharkey with, "What you aim to do to me, Tom? What you trying to do?"

Advancing years, precarious employment, and near-poverty did not dull Johnson's zest for life, nor lessen his interest in national affairs. As we have seen, politicians walked warily around Johnson; this did not prevent him from backing a Presidential candidate before the Universal Negro Improvement Association at Detroit when Franklin D. Roosevelt ran for a second term. Johnson said, "Mr. Roosevelt is champion now and wearing the belt. Abraham Lincoln was a good fighter in his prime, but he can't help us now. Always string along with the champion."

Though his man won the election, no rewards came to

Johnson, and two years later he was glad to accept a walk-on role as a captured Ethiopian general in a New York Hippodrome production of *Aida*. He made a fine appearance in his leopard skins, but the pay was mostly in publicity. Before the performance, Johnson said to a reporter, "They needed a big strong fellow, and black—and that was me. I am to be the head general of Ethiopia, dressed up like Selassie with robes and all, and they take me up to Memphis—not Memphis, Tennessee, but in the old country—and I am a prisoner. So I've got to struggle. Boy, I mean to struggle plenty."

"Do they put you in chains?" he was asked.

"They are supposed to and I expect they'll try to," Johnson replied. "If they can get chains on me, okay and good, but I got to show up well. I can't be a ninny!" He then shifted the conversation and said that the reason he beat Jeffries was because he was a Republican. "Roosevelt! Roosevelt!" Johnson cried. "He has done more for the black race than Lincoln!"

In this kind of clowning, Johnson showed the surface personality he had developed in his mature years. And yet an observer might wonder, how did he *really* feel? He probably showed that only when he got behind the wheel of an automobile. It required no psychiatrist to sense the anger and arrogance expressed in the speeds at which his big cars rushed along the roads. The extraordinary quickness of Johnson's reflexes—plus good luck—had always saved him and others from injury. But as he approached the age of seventy, those marvelously fast reactions began to slow down. And though he did not admit it, his hearing and memory also began to be impaired. But so far as he could tell, the luck was still with him.

That was the situation on June 10, 1946, when Johnson crossed the border of North Carolina, heading for New York at the wheel of his Lincoln Zephyr. He was returning from an engagement with a small Texas circus, and traveling fast. Beside him sat a man named Fred L. Scott, whom he had employed to go along for company and to spell him in driving. Around 3:30 P.M., they approached the outskirts of Franklinton, about thirty miles north of Raleigh, where U.S.-1 swings in a gentle curve. A truck rose into view coming the other way. Johnson lost control of the car and it went off the shoulder to the right. He pulled back heading for the truck and wrenched the wheel, but the Zephyr yawed across the concrete and crashed into a power pole. Scott was thrown clear and escaped with minor injuries. The driver's side of the car was crumpled and Johnson was unconscious. They got him to St. Agnes' Hospital at Raleigh in less than an hour, and he died from internal injuries at 6:10 P.M.

The younger staff at the hospital did not know who their emergency patient was, but an old doctor looked down on the broad black face and said, "That's Jack Johnson."

Next day Irene Johnson sent instructions to ship Jack's body to Chicago, where it was displayed at an undertaker's on South Michigan Avenue throughout June 13, with large crowds of Negroes, a few whites among them, waiting to file past the open casket. On June 14, thousands of Negroes stood in the streets outside the big high-domed Pilgrim Baptist Church, with a corps of Red Cross workers on hand to calm the hysterical. In the auditorium 2,500 mourners listened to the eulogy by the Rev. Junius Caesar Austin.

"Jack struck a double blow when he became heavyweight champion," said the minister. "If we hadn't had a Jack, we wouldn't have a Joe now." The reference was to Joe Louis, who then held the heavyweight title. "Jack was a hard, clean fighter," the pastor went on. "He never hit below the belt. And he was the hardest hitter of his generation." True enough; but it was observed that not even a floral wreath had come from a fighter, black or white, young or old, and that no delegation of boxers had appeared at the church.

They buried Johnson next to Etta in the old and peacefully landscaped Graceland Cemetery on North Clark Street. He lies among the tombs of Ryersons, Ishams, Palmers, and McCormicks, near the tall column that marks the resting place of George M. Pullman. A towering oak casts ample shade over Jack's monument, which is a stark and massive granite block. It carries one word:

JOHNSON

From a little distance in the quiet of Graceland a visitor would take Johnson's gravestone to be that of a Chicago merchant or manufacturer, a blameless wife at his side. In these surroundings the applause is gone, and with it the bitterness of disapproval; we remember only how he stayed warm in the hearts of people who needed something to admire. For them he was a champion in the primary sense of the word: "One who acts or speaks in behalf of a person or a cause; a defender." A man could do a great deal worse than that; and on those terms, Johnson deserves his monument.

Index

* No information available.

PICTURE ACKNOWLEDGMENTS

1. Brown Brothers
2. United Press International Photo
3. Brown Brothers
4. Brown Brothers
5. Brown Brothers
6. United Press International Photo
7. Brown Brothers
8. Brown Brothers
9. Brown Brothers
10. Brown Brothers
11. Brown Brothers
12. Brown Brothers
13. Brown Brothers
14. United Press International Photo
15. Brown Brothers
16. United Press International Photo